Discovering Super-Natural Love

© 2020 by Lark Syrris

Table of Contents

Dedication

This book is dedicated to my husband Demitri Syrris whose lifetime of support and devotion has taught me to trust love, my daughter Katrina Syrris who has been my editing partner and who has inspired and awed me with her many gifts since she was born, my son, Constantine Syrris whose smile lights up even the darkest of days, and to all my fellow travelers on this spiritual pilgrimage to strengthen our ability to love.

Introduction

My spiritual quest began when I was four years old. It was triggered by the sudden death of my mother. At the time, I had no one to turn to for help in processing my grief. Both my mother and my father were atheists, so I had no notions of God or an afterlife of any kind. My mother was just gone, forever. Others outside our family made mention of Heaven (and Hell), but I found no solace from their religious platitudes.

Every night I cried myself to sleep, but, one night, my mother appeared at the foot of my bed, smiling radiantly. She assured me her love would be with me always, and she would be watching over me. She encouraged me to sleep, and although I tried as hard as I could to stay awake for fear of losing her again, I eventually did fall asleep under the warmth of her sun.

As tempted as I was, even then, to believe this paranormal encounter had just been my imagination, I needed to search for better answers, and as I grew older, I continued to have paranormal experiences I could not deny were as real as the hair on my head.

I became a voracious reader of books on psychology, theology, and philosophy from the ancient worlds to the new world. I visited different churches and temples. I took different theology classes from every perspective, and I read about psychics such as Edgar Cayce. I dabbled in New Age philosophies and pondered the universe from both the scientific and spiritual perspectives. I have spent a lifetime with my head in the clouds and my feet firmly planted in the earth, trying to understand my mystical experiences.

At this time in my life, I can say with conviction there exists a divine force of love in the universe so great it cannot be measured, but so intensely personal it cannot be ignored. Yet, many try to ignore it, to their detriment. To brush away this great love is to miss out on the grandest, most joyful, and miraculous adventure ever! I call this divine love "super-natural" because I experience it as a super power that is also as natural as the current of a river and the air we breathe. It is not beyond ordinary human experience. Super-natural love is an intricate part of our experience, and it is always there, waiting for us to acknowledge it and be willing to receive its many gifts.

To understand super-natural love, imagine you are sitting alone on a beach, looking out at the ocean, mesmerized by the clear blue waves, the warmth of the setting sun, and the comfort of the soft sand. You are fully present in this moment. No thoughts come to mind other than awareness of being here, feeling the gentle caress of the ocean breeze on your face, tasting the salty-sweet air, listening to the rhythmic lapping of the waves, and looking out at the rose and orange clouds as the sun slowing sets into the horizon. You feel safe and loved. In an instant, you realize you are one with the ocean, the sun, the wind, and the sand. In fact, you belong to all of nature, the whole human family, and the entire universe. You feel amazed and elated, as your awareness rises to the ultimate epiphany that you are even one with the divine love called, God. Now you understand what this means: no matter where you are, you are home. There is nothing to fear. All is well.

As you walk away from the beach, you know you are taking the ocean, the sun, the sand, and the love of the entire universe with you, and they will never leave you. They reside in you and are all around you. You and all of life are interconnected. The universe is in you, as you are in the universe. You share the same divine and loving energy just as everyone on this planet breathes the same air.

Super-natural love is the divine energy in the universe that has the power to create, transform, protect, and heal. It is experienced as the peaceful bliss we come to know through all our senses, including our sixth-sense. It has an infinite variety of manifestations and expressions, but always it is gentle, kind, and reassuring, reminding us there is nothing to fear. Whatever lies ahead, this miraculous love will be there to see us through. All we have to do is open the door and let it in.

In this book, I invite you to join me on my never-ending spiritual adventure with super-natural love. This book is the first of three books. All three are a collection of personal essays that will take you on my journey from discovering and connecting to super-natural love to becoming a source of super-natural love. It is my sincerest wish that reading about my spiritual adventures will inspire you to embark on your own spiritual quest, feeling free to question, to shed out-worn beliefs that are not working for you anymore, and to find your own soul's callings and convictions that will drive your life forward to ever greater joy, peace, and miracles.

CHAPTER 1

MY FIRST ENCOUNTER WITH SUPER-NATURAL LOVE

When I was four years old, my mother died from complications of a surgery to remove an ovarian cyst. The surgery was considered to be low risk, so no one anticipated that she would have convulsions during recovery and die.

My family experienced the normal stages of grief, but we were not allowed to talk about it. Adults in that time considered children to be too young, and, frankly, stupid, to be as affected by such events as adults, a belief that I heard stated many times, "Children are resilient. They don't understand." This was 1961, an era in which the common knowledge of psychology was limited to a nod to Freud, which in itself was limited to having heard about him at some dinner party. Simply, psychology was considered irrelevant, useless, and only good for an occasional entertaining conversation.

I was considered to be too young to attend my mother's funeral, so the reality of her death took some time to completely register. However, I did understand what death meant, and I knew when I heard the news, I would never see her again, a realization made worse by the fact that the last time I had seen her, I had thrown a temper fit over having to clean my room, and I slapped her in the face. The last time I saw her face, she had been looking at me with silent shock and disappointment. No further words were exchanged between us. I never had the chance to tell her, "I love you." I was never able to tell her I was sorry. I would never be able to thank her for loving me. I would not even have the chance to say, "Good-bye."

I was not allowed to speak of this. I suffered the guilt and anguish alone. When I was left alone in the dark of night in bed, I cried, I whispered, "I'm so sorry," and I trembled until my body became exhausted and finally collapsed into sleep.

I had not been acquainted with the idea of God or the afterlife because my parents were atheists. There were no such magical ideas taught in our household. So, on the night when my crying was interrupted by the soft sounds of a symphony playing a minuet, I sat up in bed wondering who was playing music. The ballroom music floated through my bedroom, and a light shone softly on the menagerie of figurines standing high on glass shelves on the wall facing me. The light seemed to breathe life into the figurines, and the glass shelves became their dance floors. The lady figurines waltzed around, their gowns swirling pink, blue, and yellow. The Indian brave danced with the pilgrim girl, his dark braids glistening like moonbeams, gently brushing across the girl's ruffles and lace. I watched them smile and bow to one another and felt their delight.

Suddenly, the music stopped, and the dancers returned to their original positions and stood still. In that same moment, my mother appeared, standing at the foot of my bed, smiling warmly at me. She was as radiant as the sun. She told me she loved me, not to be afraid or worried, and she would always be watching over me. She encouraged me to sleep, and I felt a peaceful drowsiness overcome me, even though I tried with all my might to stay awake for fear of losing her again. Her radiant warmth overcame me, and I eventually fell asleep. When I awoke the next morning, she was gone.

Although I was tempted to believe I had just imagined my mother had visited me, I felt certain she had been there. I didn't understand how something like this could happen, but I knew deep in my soul it happened, and I knew I was loved, absolutely, unconditionally, and forever. I yearned to share this experience with my brothers and my father. I wished they too could be comforted by it, and I wondered if they might have had a similar experience. I ran to the breakfast table and shouted, "I saw Mom last night!" They looked at me with smug smiles and told me I had just been dreaming. I knew then that if I had tried to convince them it was real, they would have just laughed at me or patted me on the head in the same way one pats the family dog and walks away. I knew I was better off to return to my own magical world, without them.

I have had several paranormal experiences since that night, which have persuaded me that what is called, "supernatural" is actually natural when we have open minds and hearts and are receptive to all the divine energy around us and within us. Just because an experience cannot be explained, measured, or repeated, does not mean it is not real. Just a little bit of humility with the understanding we don't know it all can lead us to the greatest love and the best adventures we could never have imagined before.

Experiencing the paranormal is easier for young children who have not yet been fully indoctrinated to close their minds. To a young child, anything is possible. All the world is still a marvel. I had been receptive to the paranormal because I did not know it was not supposed to happen. I had not yet been fully instructed on what is regarded as real and what is not, so every experience was equally real for me.

As a young child, I had no pride in my knowledge. In fact, I assumed I knew nothing. I was naturally humble. World-weary adults are another story. Most have difficulty with humility. We have a tendency to believe we have seen it all, and we know it all. Most of us have lost our natural curiosity long ago, and our indoctrination, albeit religious or secular, has closed our minds. Without humility, we cannot take in new information. If we believe we know all the answers, we will cease asking questions. How can we learn something new if we believe we already know everything?

The key to opening a closed mind is humility. To cultivate, humility, the first step is to give yourself permission to question everything you have been taught:

- Is there anything you have been taught that does not make sense when you compare it to your experience?
- Is your current world view working for you?
- Do your current beliefs help you to be happy or to have positive relationships?
- What might be missing from your world view?
- Have you ever had an experience that your current understanding of reality cannot explain?
- How did that experience feel to you?
- Did it bring you peace or did it frighten you?
- What was life like for you when you were a child?
- What experiences comforted you?
- Who loved you and inspired you?
- How would you explain your own experiences with love?
- Is love real? How do you know?
- If love, intangible and unmeasurable, is real, then could super-natural love be real too?

All new learning begins with a question and an open, receptive mind. If you want to discover super-natural love, choosing to believe it is possible will open the door to a peaceful visitor bearing the gift of Heaven on Earth.

CHAPTER 2

MY FIRST SPIRITUAL TEACHER

As I reflected on my paranormal encounter with my mother, I realized how much I had needed to see her smiling because the last time I had seen her face, she was looking at me with profound disappointment, and that memory tortured me. I hated myself. I blamed myself for her death. I thought maybe she chose to die because I had been mean to her. As a four-year-old girl, I didn't know any better.

Somehow, my mother, now completely immersed within the divine energy of the universe, knew I needed her reassurance to begin to heal from my grief. And somehow, she appeared to me for just that purpose, to reassure me she still existed somewhere in the vast unknown, she was okay, she still loved me, and I would be okay too.

When she was alive, my mother had been nothing but kind to me, and she was the only person who had conversations with me. I was the youngest child, and she spent all her days caring for me while my brothers were in school. My entire life at that time had been all about her. She had been my whole world, and when she died, she took my world with her. How would I spend my days now? Who would sing with me at the piano? Who would take me for walks in the woods? Who would lift me up when I fell? Who would teach me, encourage me, hug me, and keep me company? I missed my mother, and having learned that she still existed somewhere else made me want to go there to be with her.

Our family cat, Tiger, was my only companion. He allowed me to hold on to him for dear life any time of day or night. Tiger had the patience of a saint, allowing me to haul him with me everywhere and dress him up in doll clothes. He seemed to know it was his purpose to be with me. He came to sleep with me every night, and his warm affection and purring lulled me to sleep.

Soon, there came a new companion, our nanny. Mrs. Hansen was a soft-spoken elder with pure white hair. With her guidance, daily life settled into a predictable routine. I came to love Mrs. Hansen, and I trusted her because I felt she loved me too. She took an interest in me, and she knew, for example, how much I depended on Tiger for companionship. On one summer day, I decided Tiger had to be wherever I was, and I got the idea to tie a long piece of twine around his neck to use as a leash. I pulled him out the front door to take a walk with me. Suddenly, I heard Mrs. Hansen rush out the door behind me and call my name. I stopped and turned around to hear her. She gently approached me and asked, "Do you love Tiger?"

I responded, "Of course I do! That's why I want him to be with me all the time."

She said, "If you love Tiger, take that rope off his neck, because if you don't, you're going to kill him!"

I was shocked, but I quickly obeyed. Then Mrs. Hansen said, "You have to trust that Tiger loves you too, and let him choose to be with you. If he ever chooses to do something else, then you just let him, and trust that he will come back to you."

Mrs. Hansen was a gentle old soul, but she was feisty too.

One morning, when my brothers were doing their farm chores, the ram cut loose from his pen and chased my eldest brother from the barn all the way up the steep hill and straight through the front door of our house. I saw Mrs. Hansen run to my brother's aid. With only a broom for a weapon, she threw herself at that wild and angry ram. I watched her white locks of hair flying furiously as she repeatedly wacked the ram with the broom, shouting, "Shoo!" She pushed that big-horned ram back out the door. The ram didn't know what had hit him, but he finally calmed down enough for my brother to lead him back to the barn.

Then there was the night we nearly lost our Mrs. Hansen when she lost her patience with us. My father must have been out on a date because Mrs. Hansen wasn't normally with us after dinner. That night we had pushed her beyond her limits. We were watching TV when suddenly my brothers decided to pick a fight, first with each other, then with me, grabbing my doll and playing keep away with it. I cried and screamed at them to give it back, but the more I cried, the more they laughed. Mrs. Hansen told them several times to stop, but they wouldn't. We must have shredded her every nerve because she finally shouted, "That's enough!" Then she grabbed her purse and keys and slammed the door behind her. We all jumped to the window and watched her drive down the driveway.

My eldest brother ran out the front door and chased after her, shouting, "We're sorry, Mrs. Hansen, please come back!" She stopped her car and rolled down her window. I couldn't hear what they said to one another, but my brother must have promised he would behave because she came back. I don't believe she spoke a word of this trouble to our father because we never heard a word of it again. She must have forgiven us and decided to let it go.

I regard Mrs. Hansen as my first spiritual teacher. Through her example, she taught me about the nature and importance of love. From her I learned love involves taking a genuine interest in someone, listening, teaching, and sharing. She taught me love requires trust, and it respects free will, even the free will of the family pet. From her, I learned love nurtures, protects, and forgives.

Finally, Mrs. Hansen taught me how to pray to that divine universal energy she called, "God." I still remember my most earnest and secret prayer. Lying in bed at night, I put my little hands together, palm to palm, and I prayed, "God, please show me how to help people. I don't want any other girl or boy to hurt like me." Then I would quietly sing a song Mrs. Hansen had taught me, "All night, all day, angels watching over me, my Lord...." The prayer, the melody, the rhythm, and the thought of angels protecting me were soothing, and I fell asleep, feeling safe and loved.

Little by little, day by day, I entered the acceptance stage of grief, finding peace and healing through the sheer grace of the love that came to me through every act of kindness and caring, from the paranormal visit from my mother's spirit, to Tiger the cat, and to Mrs. Hansen. I discovered life here on Earth is still worth living, full of pleasant surprises and lessons to be learned, and the best lesson of all was I am not alone. Life can be at times excruciatingly painful, but love, if we let it, will see us through to better and happier days.

I have applied the lessons I learned from Mrs. Hansen every day for the remainder of my life. I am forever grateful to her. I am grateful for the love she gave me and that had brought her to me. She gave me my will to live, my life's purpose, and the basic tools I needed to build my foundation of faith and my relationship with the miraculous force of super-natural love that has sustained me ever since she walked through our front door and into my heart.

CHAPTER 3

BUILDING A FOUNDATION OF FAITH

Throughout my childhood, I had been confronted with two opposite world views: my father's atheism and the town's version of Christianity, neither of which appealed to me. My father's view completely dismissed my spiritual experiences, and the town's view of God felt completely wrong. Certainly, their preaching of Hell and damnation and the "chosen few" did not fit my experience with super-natural love as an all-inclusive force in the universe.

Mine was not a punishing and wrathful God who threw people into the flames of eternal Hell if they didn't obey Him. My God was not a man. My God was an enigmatic, but undeniable experience that came from love and was expressed through love, and love was never cruel or demanding. Rather, it was soft-spoken, unimposing, and gentle. My God became known to me through a quiet inner voice, an intuition, and peaceful, reassuring experiences that gave me the sense that all is well and will be well. My God was a purely loving energy that flowed to me and through me. It never judged or condemned me or anyone else. It did not bully or intimidate or make demands to follow a set of rigid rules. It was not self-serving, expecting to be worshipped like a narcissistic king. My God would not put my mother and father or anyone I knew in a horrible place called Hell. In fact, I knew, from my paranormal visit with my deceased mother that she was indeed somewhere in the universe, but it certainly was not Hell because her spirit was overflowing with love and joy.

My father's atheism was no secret. Every chance he got, and everywhere he went, he made a point to declare his disbelief. Whenever the subject of religion arose, he would ask, "How can you believe in an invisible man upstairs pushing buttons?" His confrontational atheism made him the target of priests, nuns, ministers, and pastors who felt they were called to convert this ornery farmer to save his soul. All of them drove miles out of their way to our house on the farm on a regular basis for this mission. When they came to our door with Bibles in hand, my father politely dismissed them. But that didn't stop them from trying again on another day.

The most memorable occasions involved frustrated preachers who pulled me aside to persuade me to persuade my father to convert. They told me that if I didn't help them to get through to my father, he would burn in eternal Hell. I, being a child, might be spared this fate, but if I did not declare a belief in their man, Jesus, by the time I was an adult, I too would burn in Hell.

Their audacity to threaten me like this rendered me speechless. However, had I been able to speak during these ludicrous encounters, I would have told them I didn't know their man, Jesus, and if he was intending to torture my family and me forever in a horrific prison called Hell, I had no interest in getting to know him.

For me, building a foundation of spiritual faith became an exploratory process with the aim to sort through all the influences from home and from society and deciding which were worth keeping, and which should be discarded. It involved investigating the various belief systems in the world and giving myself the freedom to question. In the end, my faith in super-natural love came from trusting my own intuition and common sense to discern the difference between true and false, right from wrong, and fake from genuine. The exploratory process became a lifetime of reading about all the major religions, philosophies from the ancient Greeks to Ralph Waldo Emerson, anthropology, archeology, world history, and literature from everywhere in the world. I visited churches and temples. I took several theology classes. I dabbled in New Age literature, and I took an interest in mystics and psychics such as Edgar Cayce. I also took an interest in science and quantum physics. Darwin's theory of evolution made sense to me, and I did not see it as a way to disprove the existence of God. His theory simply describes how life on Earth evolved. It didn't say anything about the ultimate source of life, and contrary to popular opinion, Darwin mentioned the importance of love to our survival far more often than he mentioned the idea of the survival of the fittest. Quantum physics describes the miracle of energy, which seems to be getting closer to proving the existence of God more than disproving. I never saw a dichotomy between science and spirituality. I have come to see they go together nicely. Science teaches how to think logically whereas spirituality teaches us about love and ethics. Science without ethics would result in the destruction of the world. Spirituality without logic results in dangerous dogma that promotes hate and "holy" wars.

Over the years, I have discovered what speaks to my own spiritual awakening and what does not. The Native American sacred regard for nature, spoke to my experience of communing with God in the meadows and woods and feeling the soulfulness within animals. Buddhism and Hinduism spoke to my sense of peace that I felt when praying or meditating, as well as my sense of having lived before in previous lives. The New Testament spoke to my experience of God as a miraculous power of love, and the Rabbi, Jesus, as I came to understand him, turned out to be nothing like the man the preachers of my childhood made him out to be. I had to wonder if they had ever actually read the New Testament because they certainly did not come to the same understanding of Jesus that I did.

I did not come away from my readings and studies of the New Testament with the idea that Jesus represented the irrational and narcissistic God the preachers of my childhood spoke about. In fact, I came to understand Jesus as a rebel against such an idea of God, which had come from the depiction of God in the Old Testament. Jesus had to have been fully aware of this Old Testament idea of God as a jealous and random tyrant, much like the ancient Egyptian, Greek, and Roman Gods of mythology. Jesus's disdain for this idea of God is why he argued so much with the Pharisees, who were the equivalent of priests in his time. Jesus taught the opposite idea of God. He described God as a father figure who is kind and forgiving and who, like most any human father, only wants his children to be happy and well. Jesus's God was a father who suffers when he sees his children suffer and seeks to make them well again, just as Jesus wept for his friends and dedicated his life to healing others. This was an entirely new idea of God, or at least a new emphasis on a loving and healing God as opposed to a demanding and demeaning tyrant.

My understanding of Jesus now is of a man who knew better than anyone else the miraculous power of love, which comes through faith in the divine love that he called, "Father", who, when asked, will assist us in manifesting miracles through his holy spirit. My interpretation of this teaching is simply, God, called by any name, Father, Mother, Holy Spirit, or Great Spirit, is simply super-natural love that is willing and able to help us to transcend what scientists call the laws of nature to manifest miracles. Jesus taught this super-natural love is available to anyone who seeks it or asks for it with the faith that in their seeking, they shall find it, and in their asking, they shall receive it. Whenever he healed someone, he commented on that person's faith as having been a prerequisite of the healing. In one case, he even expressed surprise at a woman's faith, and exclaimed, ""Woman, you have great faith! Your request is granted," (Matthew 15:28. International Standard Bible).

I believe Jesus served as both a conduit and a teacher of the divine, loving, universal energy that is called God. He may have even been the incarnation of God, but I believe Jesus was teaching us that we all can be the incarnation of God if we choose to learn and apply his teaching to have faith, to develop a close relationship with the same divine energy with which he was intimate, and to act with love in all our daily interactions with others. Jesus taught us how to love and how to become one with the divine loving energy of the universe. He taught us that to live with this energy inside of us is the way to manifest a joyful, peaceful and heavenly existence, and, conversely, to live without this loving energy leads to misery and despair—a hellish existence. We choose and manifest our own realities. If we choose to manifest hate, we will live in a cruel reality. If we choose to manifest love, we will live in a kind and peaceful reality, not just in the afterlife, but also here and now in this life. Finally, Jesus taught us not to fear death, for we, like him, will be resurrected into a new life after this life. He taught us that our soul's energy lives eternally, in one form or another.

Jesus was way ahead of his time, already having figured out what quantum physicists are just now discovering, over 2000 years later. How did Jesus figure it out? Pardon the pun, but only God knows. Jesus was a very special man indeed, and, somehow, perhaps through many previous life incarnations, or perhaps through being the very essence of the entire divine universal energy that is God, he knew what has always been, with no beginning and no end.

What I found through all my exploration of both Eastern

and Western religious beliefs and texts was a common thread--an emphasis on compassion and respect for all of life. I also found a lot of irrational, contradictory, divisive, and obscure messages that did not support the values of compassion and respect. Anything that supported and enriched my ability to be a more loving and empowered person I added to my spiritual foundation. Anything that led to divisive and hurtful attitudes and behaviors I discarded. I knew what kind of person I wanted to be, and I knew only love could heal us and manifest the kind of peaceful reality where I wanted to live.

After building my own eclectic spiritual foundation, the only question that remained was how to love in a tangible and practical sense, and how to love when it seems impossible in the face of the challenges of daily life. I learned love is not just a feeling. It is an active force that can change everything. It can even perform miracles, and it starts with the choice to love and to be loved.

CHAPTER 4

THE POWER OF INFLUENCE

In the 1970s, I had witnessed a close friend with whom I had grown up shed his original personality and take on an entirely new, and to me, alien, personality during his early adulthood, seemingly overnight. During his teen years, he had been popular, a ham on stage, a very talented drummer in a band, and he hung out with creative, friendly, and amusing friends. Rock and Roll was his favorite music, and the Beatles, his favorite rock band. Unlike several of his friends who had decided to go to college, my friend had decided to get married to his high school sweetheart. He took a conventional job to support his wife, who had decided to be a stay-at-home wife, with the intention of someday having children.

His wife kept their home clean and organized, and she cooked their meals, while my friend went to work at his job. They led a traditional lifestyle in every way. While visiting with them one evening, I noticed they were playing "elevator music" on the radio. It was dull with no hint of talent, soul, or passion. My friend would have abhorred such music not even a year prior to this evening. In addition to giving up his music, he appeared to have given up everything that had been interesting and fun about him. Physically, he looked the same, but I felt like something strange had possessed him and taken over his body.

I mentioned to my friend all the differences I saw in him, including his current taste in music and his mannerisms, and I asked him what had happened. He smiled, somewhat smugly, and said, "I've been born again."

"What does that mean?" I asked. At this time in my life, I really had no idea what he was talking about.

"It means, I'm saved. Jesus saved me, and my old self is gone," he responded.

"I was not aware you needed to be saved. What was wrong with who you were?" I asked.

He didn't respond, except to say he was so much happier now that he had found his Lord and Savior.

I decided to explore this strange phenomena and learn more about my friend's beliefs. Throughout several conversations, I learned that he believed all humans are born worthless sinners who will perish in eternal Hell if they do not accept Jesus Christ as their Lord and Savior. This belief was familiar to me. It was the same belief all the ministers, priests, and nuns had preached on the doorstep of our farm house during their failed attempts to convert my atheist father.

Apparently, my friend had been convinced that who he was before he was "born again" had been worthless and deserving of the eternal flames of Hell. His condemnation of his former identity confused me. As far as I knew, he had never harmed anyone, and certainly, if he had, never to the point of deserving to be damned to Hell forever.

To try to understand further, I asked my friend why he believed he was such a terrible sinner. What had he done that I might not have known about? But, rather than answer that question, my friend just stated the same belief repeatedly: we are all sinners, regardless, because we were born in "original sin". We were born this way because Eve seduced Adam into eating the forbidden fruit in the Garden of Eden, and now we must all pay for their sins.

I felt like Alice in Wonderland, thinking, "Curious and curiouser" every time either my friend or his wife attempted to explain how they arrived at their beliefs. At last, I was persuaded to attend their church, which identified itself as evangelical, non-denominational Christian. The congregation expressed their belief that it was their job to spread the gospel and save souls. Their minister preached a sermon about how the members of this church were the "chosen few" who would go to Heaven because they were superior to all other Christian churches as well as all other religions. Then he preached about all the books and movies that were on his banned list and why they were evil influences.

At this point, the preacher touched a personal nerve with me. He dismissed the character, Zorba, from one of my favorite books and movies, *Zorba the Greek*, as nothing more than a "perverted old man." After which, he preached that education in general was evil, and any book that was not the Bible was suspect. It became blatantly clear this man was throwing hate all over the place, hatred toward the educated and hatred toward anyone who was in any way different from himself, including people who attended other types of Christian churches.

I remained inside this church as long as my stomach could take it. I did not want to offend or disrespect my friend and his wife, but, at last, I had to leave. I felt too sick to tolerate any more of this hate speech.

I waited for my friend and his wife in the church parking lot. When they came out of the church, full of smiles, I did not know what to do with them. All I could tell them was I had felt sick and had to leave. I knew it was useless to explain to them that their preacher taught hate instead of love. They had already been so thoroughly overcome by this hateful dogma that any attempt I might have made to explain my perspective would have been a futile exercise of banging my head against a wall.

Over the years, I tried to visit with my friend several more times after this event, and I tried to steer clear from all conversation about religion. However, he and his wife saw my every visit as an opportunity to preach to me and save my soul. After several of our discussions turned into heated arguments, I realized it was time to part ways and never return. They had condemned me to Hell for so many reasons I lost count. I was going to Hell because I was an educated woman, and women are not supposed to be educated. I was going to Hell because I delayed having children. Women should not have careers, and so it was, on and on.

I came to the conclusion my friend and his wife had lost their minds to this church, and the more I tried to help them to recover their minds, the more they condemned me to Hell. Conversation was futile. They had no genuine interest in me as a person. I was merely the object of their preaching, and they had no other life but preaching. For that matter, they had no genuine interest in themselves as people. They had become preaching robots. The only human quality that remained in them, it seemed to me, was puffed up pride in being members of the "chosen few."

My Greek husband once remarked, "The Greeks have a saying: If you go to bed with the blind, you will wake up cross-eyed." It is an interesting expression, meaning, beware of the influences in your life.

We live in a world of infinite influences, from the people we see every day to the media we see everywhere. We are inundated with propaganda, some that is artfully posing as news. We are assaulted by advertising in every form. There is always someone trying to sell us something.

To be careful about the influences you allow to enter into your heart and mind, I suggest you hear and read everything with a questioning mind. Some helpful questions include, does it make sense? How does it feel? Does it feel wrong or right? Does it inspire love or hate? Does it empower or disempower? Does it put others down to make themselves feel superior? Does it make you feel inferior? Do you sense a hidden agenda? Does the influence feel sincere or fake? Does it uplift or drag you down? Finally, does it help you to be a better, stronger, and more loving person?

I suggest choosing the influences in your life with great care. Influences become beliefs, and beliefs drive our every choice and behavior. I recommend putting everyone and every idea to the test before letting them take up space in your mind, heart, or soul. Take no one or anything for face value. Be observant, be mindful, and be free to be true to yourself.

I am not suggesting we should be closed off from new ideas or refuse to change our minds to embrace a better idea than we might have had before. Rather, I'm just saying, test every idea and every person before you let them in. Whether we like it or not, we are all under someone's influence, but we can, at least, choose our influences and give ourselves permission to let go of influences that are harmful to us and gather influences that are good for us.

Cutting ties with my close friend from childhood had not been easy. I felt guilty for giving up on him. I experienced sleepless nights wondering what had happened to him and what could I do to help him and bring him back to his authentic self. It had become clear to me that he had joined a cult that had taken possession of his mind, and I was no match for their influence. After many years of trying to reconnect with my friend, I came to feel the weight of his toxic condemnation of me, and I had to let go. Trying to hold on to the friendship did neither of us any good. The person he was when we were growing up together was no longer there, and I had to accept I would not find him.

Letting go of people who have become toxic to our mental, emotional, and spiritual health can be one of the most painful things we do, especially when these people have been close friends or relatives. We may have to endure a period of time alone and learn to be content with our solitude, keeping only our own company. However, the alternative of keeping toxic influences in our life can mean a lifetime of pain, as opposed to a temporary period of being alone. It is better to take some time to regroup and seek out new and better relationships. Have faith, and you will find them. Be true to your authentic self, and people who can appreciate you will be drawn to you as well. Good friends are those who see the good in you and encourage you to be your best self, and they will appreciate the same from you. They are worth waiting for.

The years that followed after ending my toxic friendship, I found true friends who accept me for who I am, and we mutually support each other through our daily challenges and ups and downs. We treat each other with respect, and we give each other a warm welcome whenever we meet. These friends have become members of my family, and the best part is, no matter how much we might disagree on any topic, none of us condemn anyone to Hell.

C HAPTER 5

THE REAL JESUS

One cannot live in the United States for long without an inevitable encounter with people who identify as Christians and who believe it is their purpose in life to spread the Gospel. The subject of Jesus cannot be avoided. His name is everywhere, even on billboards and bumper stickers. He seems to be a product no different from Coca Cola. His name is treated as a commodity, and there are many people who pay a large portion of their incomes to belong to churches or to be in the audience of a televised church. Jesus is possibly the most controversial subject in America, even more than the president.

When the play, *Godspell*, opened on Broadway in 1971, it stirred up the Jesus controversy more than ever before. Many Christians were offended because Jesus was portrayed as a clownish hippie, and his disciples were portrayed as flower children resembling the hippies of the 1960s. For some among the audiences, the controversy itself might have drawn them in to see the play. For others, the music might have been the draw, and, for others, maybe it was just the novelty of seeing Jesus portrayed within a contemporary context. For whatever reason, the play drew large audiences, and it still does.

I saw the play at a local dinner theater with a friend in 1974. We were joined by several strangers sharing the table, and among them was a United States senator. He was around 50 years old, and he had a somewhat antisocial demeanor, which made him the odd man out. He had come to the show by himself. His crass comments during dinner made me wonder what had brought him to the show. He didn't seem particularly interested in religion or anything spiritual. He didn't appear all that interested in musical theater either. He didn't know anyone in the show. It was like the senator had come just because he had nothing better to do, which might have been the case. The senator didn't talk much, but when he did, his manner was smug, and his responses were brief. He had a frown that seemed to be a permanent fixture on his face, which made him unapproachable.

I couldn't help but find this senator interesting, especially the mystery he brought to my mind as to why he was there when he didn't seem to want to be there. Occasionally during the show, I glanced in his direction to see his reaction. He was poker faced throughout, and I could not discern whether or not he was enjoying the show.

My friend and I enjoyed the high energy of the actors and the music. We also felt the poignancy of the story, which seemed more like a love story among friends than a didactic sermon. Although the script was, for the most part, the text of the Book of Matthew, this delivery of the teachings brought to light the humanity of Jesus better than the New Testament text alone could. So, it was no surprise when the audience shed tears as they gave the performers a standing ovation at the end of the show, but I did not expect the senator's reaction. When I looked in his direction, he was so overcome by emotion, he could not stand up. Instead, he remained seated in his chair and wept. Given his antisocial demeanor before the play, to say I was surprised would be an understatement.

I sat down next to the senator and said nothing. I decided this man should not be left alone. After he had calmed down, I asked him if he was okay. He dabbed his eyes with a napkin and said he would be fine. I didn't know what else to say to him. It seemed to me the man had undergone a spiritual transformation within the last two hours. He must have had some sort of epiphany, as though he had just met the real Jesus and was overcome by his spirit of love. In the amount of time it takes to cook a good meal, the senator had been transformed from an arrogant and mean-spirited man into a humble gentleman. I had never seen anything like this before. He didn't open up to me as to why he had been so affected by this play, and I didn't pry. All I know is this Jesus story, told in this manner, moved a mountain.

Thirty years later, a community theater asked me to help them to produce *Godspell*, and it turned out to be another mysterious experience, back stage, on stage, and within the audience. During rehearsals, the cast began to have paranormal experiences. They became convinced the theater was haunted. Every time they rehearsed the last supper scene, the radiator started clanging loudly. One actor confessed to another that she was afraid Jesus, and the entity causing the raucous were not happy that we were doing this show. Another actor responded, "Why should the noise mean that? Maybe it means the spirit is applauding." She suggested that if they asked Jesus to stop the knocking of the radiator when they were performing, and if their prayer was answered, they could take it as a sign that Jesus was actually happy with the show. They did make this request in a prayer, and the radiator never knocked again.

Another actor felt guilty for playing the role of Judas, which I did not learn until the night of the dress rehearsal. Just after the crucifixion scene had been performed, I heard a loud scream from backstage. Suddenly, "Judas" appeared, running off the stage. He exited the theater, slamming the door. Another actor came to the front of the stage and explained that "Judas" had just learned from a phone call that his sister had been killed in a car accident.

I ran after "Judas" and stopped him before he reached his car. I told him he could not drive away in this emotional state. He had to calm down first.

He shouted, "I KNEW I shouldn't have played Judas! I KNEW God would punish me! But he should have killed me, not my sister! My sister's been nothing but good! I'm the one who has done bad things!"

I approached him gently, and said, "I don't know what you've done in your life, but I can tell you that playing Judas in this play has nothing to do with this tragedy. You are not Judas. You are just playing the role of Judas to tell the Jesus story. If God did not want this story to be told, it would not be available to us. We would never have heard or read the story. Jesus would not even exist in our minds."

"Why did he take my sister? Why didn't he take me?" He responded.

"I don't know," I replied. "All I know is you are still here, and there must be a good reason—a purpose you have yet to fulfill. But, I don't think this is in any way about punishing you. And, frankly, I really can't believe you are the bad man you think you are. You have been a great cast member. You have been kind to everyone here. And I see you have made good friends."

He told me how much he loved his sister and how much he would miss her, and he cried. After he calmed down, I told him I would understand if he had to drop out of the play to take care of his family, and I allowed him to drive away.

The rest of that night and the next day, the director and I worked at a panicked pace to find a backup actor for Judas. Opening night was only a day away. How could we get any actor up to speed in time? Maybe the director himself would have to play the part. But, much to our surprise, "Judas" called and let us know he would be there on opening night.

When opening night came, "Judas" was calm. Before the

house opened, the cast expressed their condolences to him as well as their appreciation that he came back to perform. "Judas" explained what had given him the courage and the inspiration to return. He said, "My sister was the real actor. She got me into theater. Somehow, I just heard her whisper in my ear, 'Do the play! The show must go on!'" Then he smiled brightly and said, "I'm doing this for her!"

The cast cheered for "Judas" and his sister, and they gave their best performance that night. On every night of the production the audiences packed the house from the main floor to the balcony. The loving energy was electrifying in every performance.

Godspell, meaning gospel, good news, and good tidings, goes all the way back to the ancient Greek word, "euangelion," meaning good message. Why the Jesus story has had such a powerful grip on the world for so long is hard to say, but for me, the story of Jesus is the most powerful love story ever told, and to love as he loved is reward enough. It is to bring Heaven to Earth and to enjoy this life as well as whatever life might come next to the fullest. Perhaps this is why the play, *Godspell*, has so much power, even after all these years. It captures the heart of Jesus and leaves the dogma behind.

It is equally difficult to say whether there was a real Jesus, and if there was, who was he, actually? Was he a man like any man who somehow knew how to perform miracles? Or was he the one and only embodiment of God? Was he the historical, royal heir to the Jewish throne, and if it had not been for the Roman Empire, would he have been the real King of the Jews?

There is more information missing from Jesus's life story in the New Testament than is there. It leaves no clue what happened to him between the ages of 12 and 30. It doesn't say much about his upbringing or his education. Was he a member of the mainstream Hebrew religion of his time, or was he a member of the obscure and more mystical group called, the Essenes? Did he ever travel to nearby nations after his return from Egypt where he had spent his early childhood? Was he influenced in any way by the Buddhist monks who had wandered in Israel during his lifetime? Did he ever marry or have children?

There is also no way to verify what Jesus had actually said or taught. There is nothing written by his hand. All that we have are stories told by others—hearsay. The stories were first handed down through the oral tradition, and about 70 years after Jesus was said to have died, the first books of the New Testament were written, first in two languages, ancient Hebrew and Greek, then translated in Latin, and later translated in every language in the world, many times over, edited, and re-edited, interpreted and re-interpreted.

There are more Christian sects than we can count, each with their own idea of their Lord and Savior, some that emphasize his birth, others that emphasize his sacrifice, and others that emphasize his resurrection, and everyone disagreeing on what type of dogma to add to the story. But, if we look at the heart of Jesus's teachings, that is what we find—all heart. Whoever Jesus might have been or who he might be still in the spiritual realm, clearly, he cared about humanity. Through his love, people were miraculously healed. Every page in the Gospel describes a miracle he performs to help someone. Every parable in his teachings demonstrates how we should care for each other and how to have a good relationship with the divine spirit that is called God.

Perhaps it is because I live in the United States where Jesus is a major controversy that I have felt compelled to study Jesus more than any other mystic or spiritual teacher, and I have come to regard him as the greatest miracle worker who ever lived. On nearly every page of the New Testament, there is a description of Jesus working a miracle, from turning water into wine, walking on water, feeding thousands with just one loaf of bread and one fish, healing incurable diseases instantaneously, and even resurrecting the dead. His final miracle was his own resurrection from his own death.

For any educated or thinking person, opening one's mind to the possibility that Jesus's miracles actually happened can be a tough challenge. Ironically, however, it is science that is putting the proof in the pudding, so to speak. I am no expert on the subject, but I have done some research on quantum physics, and I find it fascinating. Quantum physicists have created a bridge between science and ancient spirituality, and it is this bridge, which, I believe, will eventually lead to a better understanding and acceptance of the reality of miracles. Through scientific experiments, quantum physicists have proven that everything, including all people, animals, plant life, and even inanimate objects, are made of energy, and this energy is ever moving and changing form. They have proven that the observer directly influences the results of the experiments simply by observing. In other words, quantum physicists have proven that merely focusing on something changes its energy—its form and its behavior. In addition, they have proven that an object can be in more than one place at the same time. Perhaps the greatest connection quantum physicists have made to spirituality is their scientific evidence that proves energy, the substance of all of life, never dies; it just changes form. In other words, they have proven, through scientific experiments, life is eternal.

Studies done on the mind-body connection in the psychology field are equally remarkable. Given that I am a psychotherapist, I have read many books on this subject too, but I discovered one of the most remarkable findings while listening to public radio as I was driving to work several years ago. I learned there had been a study of people suffering from depression. I did not catch who had done this research, so I cannot cite this work directly, but I can say there have been many similar studies done. According to this particular public radio announcement, people suffering from exactly the same diagnosis of depression and whose MRI brain scans revealed identical indicators of depression, were divided into three separate groups. One group was treated with psychotherapy alone, another with only antidepressant medication, and one group was not provided any treatment at all. When all three groups returned several months later, interviews were conducted with all the groups' members, and new MRI brain scans were performed. The results were astounding. Psychologists conducting the experiment discovered that the group who had been provided only psychotherapy, which was called, "talk therapy", showed the exact amount of improvement in their condition, both in their interviews and in the physicality of their brains, as did the group that had been provided only antidepressant medicine. This proved that psychotherapy alone can actually heal the brain. Lastly, the group that was not provided any treatment at all revealed their symptoms of depression had become more severe, both in their interviews and in their MRI scans. The conclusion of the study was that the best practice for treating depression would be to give patients both psychotherapy and medicine, but my conclusion as a psychotherapist was if one can be cured from depression from psychotherapy alone, then why not try that first? Medication, with all its possible side effects, should be the last resort. Certainly, however, medicine without psychotherapy is a bad idea.

The power of thought or belief has never ceased to amaze me. When I work with clients using Cognitive Behavioral Therapy (CBT), I frequently witness what I would regard as miraculous healing. When my clients choose to let go of negative beliefs and develop positive beliefs, they report significant improvements both in the way they feel and in their ability to function, and those clients who embrace a healthy sense of hope and faith in a loving force in the universe make even more significant improvements.

Could it be that Jesus was simply a man who was way ahead of his time? Could we someday learn what he knew? Could we learn to channel the energy of our love and faith to manifest miracles that defy what we now regard as the laws of nature just as Jesus had done? Could this be why Jesus had tried to teach his disciples how to perform miracles too? Could this be why Jesus had said to them, "This and more you shall do"? Could it also be why Jesus spoke as much about the importance of faith as he did about love? Could this be the ultimate message and good news Jesus had intended to share—that we too can access the divine energy within ourselves, and, with the help of God, the divine universal energy, become expert miracle workers too? I love to think so. And, truly, this good news is the only message that makes sense of Jesus.

Years before I had heard of the law of attraction, made popular by the book, *The Secret*, and by the documentary *What the Bleep Do We Know?*, I experienced what I had regarded then as amazing synchronicity. At the time, my husband and I were living in an apartment complex where every apartment had a balcony. We had just moved in, and we didn't know any of our neighbors. We were just getting adapted to our new jobs and surroundings. When I returned from work on one summer day, I happened to notice the patio furniture on a neighbor's balcony. I admired it and had a brief thought, "I would like furniture like that on my balcony." I never gave it another thought. It was not important to me. I had many other higher priorities and daily responsibilities to think about.

Several days later, someone knocked at our apartment door. I answered the door, and there stood a young man, a complete stranger, holding a chair from the balcony furniture I had silently admired for a brief moment. He said, "I brought this chair to show you my patio furniture to see if you would like to have it. I'm moving, and I can't take it with me."

I was surprised, to say the least. I had never met this man before. I had never spoken a word to him. Why did he come to me of all people? I asked him how much he wanted for it, and he said, "Oh, I'm not selling it. If you like it, you can just have it." I thanked the man profusely, and I asked him why he chose my door to knock on. Did he see me admiring this furniture several days ago? He said, "No, I never saw you before. I just had a thought pop into my head to knock on your door. I don't know why. I had no idea you had seen my furniture. That's why I brought the chair with me so you could see it." Naturally, I agreed to take it, and by the time my husband had returned from work, it was all set up nicely on our balcony.

Years later when I read about the law of attraction, the memory of this man and his balcony furniture came to mind. Was that what I had experienced? I had a thought, and the universe responded? Just like that? Or was this some sort of telepathy with the original owner of the furniture? Or, maybe, it was a combination of these forces at work. To be certain, however, this had been no mere coincidence. This event had to have occurred by design, so to speak. I will say, this experience made the idea of the law of attraction credible. Some strange magic had occurred, and I wonder how much more of such magic, perhaps more subtle, had been occurring throughout my life. Could my thoughts really have this much power to manifest my reality, like a genie in the bottle?

I reviewed my life, searching for more evidence of how my thoughts had manifested my reality, for better or for worse. According to the law of attraction, every thought is interpreted as a wish, and the universe will respond accordingly. It works that way in the mind-body connection as well. The book, *Mind as Healer; Mind as Slayer*, explains how the body interprets thoughts. For example, if we repeatedly think, "I hate my life," the body interprets this thought as a command to shut down. Conversely, if we think about how happy we are, the body responds with improved health. According to the law of attraction, we not only get what we wish for, we also get what we don't want, just because we are thinking about it. If there is any merit to the law of attraction, then, we had better become more conscious and deliberate with our thoughts. Otherwise, we might unknowingly create more misery for ourselves than we ever would have intended had we been more aware. But, the good news is, if we learn to master our thoughts and emotions, we could very well increase our odds of creating healthier and happier realities for ourselves.

As I searched for evidence of the law of attraction in my own life history, I recalled a dream I had many years before. It occurred during a time in my life when I was feeling depressed. Both my husband and I had lost our jobs. It was the first recession we experienced back in the 1980s. While we searched for new employment, we became so impoverished we had to choose between feeding our cat or ourselves. We chose the cat. I had become so depressed I began to entertain suicidal thoughts, which became the subject of my dream.

In the dream, I was standing on a river bank when a handsome man, dressed all in black, approached me. He was friendly, charming, and seductive. He took my hand to lead me down a path by the river. I asked him where we were going. He said, "I am taking you to the other side."

"What other side, what do you mean?" I asked.

The handsome man said, "Where you have asked to go."

"What did I ask? I don't remember," I replied.

The man smiled and looked deeply into my eyes and said, "You asked to die."

I was shocked, and I shouted, "What? No, no, no, no, there must be some misunderstanding. I don't want to die!"

The man let go of my hand and said, "Are you sure?"

"Yes! What do I have to do to prove it to you?" I asked, feeling panicked.

The man said, "You must love your life." Then he pointed to the sparkling river and the bank on the other side where I saw a woman standing, radiating bright white light.

I asked, "Who is she?"

The man answered, "She is life. Do you wish to go there? You are free to choose to live. If you wish to live, go there to her instead of going with me."

"Yes! Let me go there! I want to live!" I said.

The man responded, "Remember, you must love your life. If you don't, I will come back for you. I wish you well." He then disappeared, and as I was crossing the river to the woman on the other side, I woke up, and I was so grateful to be alive! I made a vow to myself I would make every effort to love my life, no matter what, and I would never again indulge in suicidal thoughts or self-pity.

I have lived true to my vow since. I thank God for my life every day, no matter how rich or poor. I also pray for help to remain cheerful. I am still striving to improve my ability to manage my thoughts and feelings, and as I teach what I know to my clients, I also learn. Frankly, some of my clients have become better masters at manifestation than I have, proving we learn best what we teach, and students can be the best teachers.

At this time in our human history, it seems to me most of us are like Dorothy from the *Wizard of Oz*, being tossed around by the storms of life, mostly unaware of whatever power we might have within ourselves to change our fates. We still have so much to learn about our hearts, our brains, and our courage. Like Dorothy, when she is given the gift of the magical shoes, we have little knowledge of our own magic. First we need to learn we have been given this divine gift, and then we need to learn how to use it for our highest good. I like to believe, someday, we all will learn to manifest our own heavens on earth, and come home to our divine selves, just as I believe Jesus did.

CHAPTER 6

THE NATURE OF MIRACLES

What is a miracle? What is not a miracle? If a phenomenon can be scientifically explained, does that mean it is not a miracle? Or, is all of life a miracle, whether or not it can be explained? Albert Einstein, said, "There are only two ways to live your life. One is as though nothing is a miracle. The other is as though everything is a miracle."

I believe there is a third way, which is more specific. I would say anything that results in love, kindness, hope, healing, or enlightenment is a miracle. Nature and all her beauty is a miracle. When I study the exquisite markings and colors of birds such as cedar wax wings, blue jays, cardinals, parrots, and snowy owls, I cannot help but think only a divine artist could have created such perfection in every little detail. Everywhere I look in nature from the sky to the earth, I see God.

Among humans, I see God in those who possess empathy and seek to help others. In every benevolent act and kind word, there is God, and in every answered prayer, I see a miracle. I believe miracles are the experience of super-natural love. They consist of the moments that amaze us and take our breath away. Neither science nor religion has anything to do with it. Simply, these are the moments that touch us so profoundly we cannot help but come to the conclusion there must be a God force of some kind, and this force is all good and all loving.

I have experienced many moments that have taken my breath away, including the birth of my daughter, my first meeting with my adopted son, the view of the sparkling blue Aegean Sea from the top of a mountain in Chios, Greece, and every perfect flower and song bird I have seen. I have experienced the sudden appearance of beautiful strangers who deliver uncanny messages or provide assistance that kept me out of harm's way, and, just as suddenly as these strangers appear, they disappear, not even walking away--just poof they are there and poof they are gone. I regard them as angels.

Miracles are manifested through ordinary people too, people who provide help or a kind word exactly when it is needed most. When my brother had only a two percent chance of survival from his heart surgery, he survived and thrived, and he is still thriving many years later, in my opinion, due to the work of good doctors and the assistance of angels who answered our prayers.

One of the most memorable miracles I've experienced happened about a week after my father died. Naturally, I was grieving, and I was feeling guilty for having persuaded him to choose to live longer than he may have wanted. He had suffered a major stroke that left him unable to swallow. Doctors had said he had a very good chance of full recovery if only he would comply with their physical therapy instructions. However, my father decided he would rather starve himself to death. Given the doctors' information and my own research, I came to the conclusion that he could recover if he wanted to. We had a heart-wrenching argument at the time. He shouted, "You're just afraid of dying!"

I shouted in response, "No, I'm not afraid of dying! I just don't think there is any reason to die prematurely!" My father thought about the research I presented to him, and he decided to have a feeding tube installed in his stomach. Sometime after, he suffered another stroke, and this time, in addition to not being able to swallow, he lost his ability to speak. I did more research, and I persuaded him to undergo two surgeries that would give him a chance to swallow and speak again. The surgeries succeeded in restoring his ability to speak, but not to swallow. Only additional physical therapy could help him with that. My father made every effort he could, but he was tired, and then he suffered another stroke.

At that point, the doctors were no longer optimistic. They candidly stated there was nothing more they could do for my father. His entire body was shutting down. They estimated he had no longer than a few weeks to live. I felt guilty for persuading him to suffer so much in his effort to stay alive. Maybe I should have allowed him to starve himself to death. If I had, his suffering would have been long over by now. He had told me he never wanted to live this long. He said he had wanted to die. For a week before he died, I spent every day in the Intensive Care unit visiting with him. I told him I was sorry. I told him I loved him. I read to him. I held his hand. At one point, the doctors told me I had to leave for an hour to give their patients time to rest. My father seemed to be sleeping already, so I left without complaint. I was a long way off to the other side of the room when I heard my father cry out for me, "Lark! Where did you go? Lark!"

I ran back to him, held his hand, and reassured him, "I'm here, Pop."

He calmed down and looked into my eyes. It suddenly occurred to me that he really never wanted to die. In fact, he was afraid of dying, and he was afraid to be alone. I felt the need to reassure him further, but how was the question. He had been a lifelong atheist. I thought about all the discussions we had over the years about spirituality and the possibility of eternal life. Would he now be receptive? I asked him, "Pop, have you ever reconsidered your belief about God and a possible afterlife?" He shook his head, "no."

"Well, Pop, please forgive me, but I feel I must tell you. I know there is life after this life. Don't ask me how I know this, I just do. Pop, you are never alone, and when you cross over to the afterlife, you will be greeted by all the loved ones who have gone before you, including your family and friends and your buddies from the war. They will be there for you, Pop, believe it or not, like it or not."

My father rolled his eyes and repeated, "Like it or not."

The next day, my father died. I wondered how he would feel when he discovered the other world in the afterlife. Would it be too much of a shock to him? Would he accept the loving welcome? I prayed for a sign that my father was okay in the afterlife. I prayed for a sign that would be so obvious I could not deny it or explain it away. A week later as I was getting dressed for work, an enormous rainbow in full and bright colors and in an entire, perfect arc, appeared on my bedroom wall and extended out to the hallway. I was astonished!

I did try to find an explanation for it. This was a purely sunny day, with not a cloud or a hint of humidity in the air. Rainbows require a mix of rain and sun, so how could this be? I searched for anything in my room that could have provided a prism that created this magnificent and perfect rainbow, and I found nothing. I sat on my bed and stared at the radiant rainbow in complete awe. I realized this must have been the sign for which I had prayed. I understood the message: my father had crossed over into the afterlife, and he was okay.

It seemed the rainbow would stay on my wall forever. I walked up to it and put my full arm through all the projected colors and observed the colors on my arm. At last, I left the room and asked my husband to come back with me to witness it, and he did. Together, we witnessed this miracle and shared our amazement. I really don't know how long the rainbow remained on the wall. It had to have been there for at least 30 minutes. Finally, I had to go to work. When I returned from work that day, it was no longer there, and I have never seen a rainbow appear on my wall again. This happened in 2009, so it has been several years since that moment, but, certainly, it is a moment I will never forget, nor will I forget the feelings it gave me—awe, love, forgiveness, joy, relief. Just remembering this moment renews my faith in super-natural love and its awesome and eternal beauty.

I did not create this miracle with my energy, but something or someone within the divine universe responded to the energy of my thoughts, feelings, and prayers, and gave me this gift. I am forever grateful and more faithful. It has been said that miracles are the evidence of God, and with this miracle, there can be no doubt. My father knows now. He has met the divine, and I still pray he is adjusting to his miraculous new life. He was, after all, a very stubborn atheist.

Whenever you feel like your heart is overflowing with love, joy, peace, hope or sheer awe, consider you are in the presence of a miracle. Whenever you receive messages that are helpful to you or some other assistance that rescues you or someone you love from harm, consider, again, you may have just received a gift from super-natural love. Miracles are the manifestation of a benevolent use of energy, which I call the divine universal energy or God.

Conversely, the moments that have the opposite effect on us, causing us to feel trauma, hate, outrage, and sick in our souls, are not miracles. They are the opposite of miracles, and they are manifested from a malevolent use of energy.

Energy, like any tool in a toolbox, can be used to manifest something helpful or something harmful, just as a hammer can be used to build a house, or it can be used as a weapon to harm someone. Those who are using their energy in ways that enhance physical, emotional, mental, or spiritual wellbeing are partaking in the manifestation of miracles. Those who use their energy to harm themselves or others in any way are partaking in the manifestation of evil, knowingly or unknowingly. It is important to note the difference and be aware of our own and others' intentions, thoughts, and feelings.

Perhaps the greatest power we have is the energy generated by our intentions, thoughts, beliefs, feelings, and prayers. If we are experiencing hateful thoughts or beliefs, we are likely to manifest negative and toxic energy and behave in ways that harm ourselves or others. If we are experiencing loving thoughts and feelings, we are likely to manifest positive and healing energy and behave in ways that help ourselves and others to be well and happy.

We may not be able to control our every circumstance, but we can learn to control our own intentions, thoughts, and feelings, and the more we master this self-control, the more we increase the odds of experiencing miracles. Every thought or belief triggers an emotion, and every emotion doubles the energy of the thought. When we take action based on the thought and feeling, we triple the energy, and when we ask the divine universal energy for help, the additional energy from the benevolent spiritual realm can become an immeasurable and inexplicable force for the good in this world.

Not all prayers or wishes are answered in ways we had hoped for. Sometimes "no" is the answer, but, with faith in the loving intentions of the divine universal energy in ourselves and others, we can choose to trust there is a higher purpose. There is one thing I know for certain: life does go on. No tragedy nor departure from this world is the final word. Love will always prevail, if not in this life, then in the next or in the next or in the one after that. Life is eternal. We have plenty of time. However, no time should be taken for granted. Each life and every moment is a grand opportunity to gain wisdom, to strengthen our faith, to improve our self-control, and to love and be loved, which is the greatest miracle of all.

CHAPTER 7

DIVINE INTERVENTION

One of the discussions I recall during a graduate class on literature was about the criteria used to categorize different genres of fiction. Given my experiences with the paranormal, I could not agree with academia's idea of realism. Any type of event in a novel that slightly veered away from a gloomy view of reality, especially in regard to divine intervention, immediately tossed a book outside the category of realism and placed it into either the genre of romance or fantasy. According to literary critics, human reality is bleak and void of experiences that inspire awe, wonder, love, and joy, and only those novels that mirror the dark side of the human condition are realistic. It's not just academia that holds such a bleak view of human experience. It seems to be widespread in Western culture in general.

No wonder many people discount the possibility of divine intervention as a real experience, and in discounting it, they live without it. Even when divine intervention actually occurs in their lives, they do not notice or acknowledge it. If they did notice it, they would probably just call it a lucky moment and never think about it again.

Conversely, those who accept the reality of miracles and believe they can call upon the divine universal energy for help, guidance, and protection, are more likely to notice the divine as an active force in their daily lives, which makes their experience of reality full of all the qualities that would be called romance or fantasy by academia. For believers, there is no such thing as luck or coincidence. Rather, there are signs, synchronicity, and mystical events, all of which they regard as the divine intervening in their lives on their behalf or on the behalf of those for whom they pray or meditate.

As I try to understand my own experiences with divine intervention, I see a wide variety of mystical and inexplicable events, some that come in answer to my prayers, some that happen serendipitously, and some that seem to be simply informing me of the existence of the divine universal energy in this life and beyond. I have been given guidance in visions, dreams, and uncanny moments of synchronicity that exceed any likely probability of occurring. They cannot be chalked off as meaningless coincidence or random luck.

Some of the paranormal experiences I've had baffle me more than others. The most baffling was a series of related events that began with a friend speaking to me in a dream through an electronic device similar to a phone. She informed me that she had just died. I felt shocked and sad and asked her how her death had happened, and she told me she had been driving during a blizzard when a driver of a snowplow did not see her car and plowed into her. She told me every detail of how the plow had hit her in the temple of her head, killing her instantly.

I told my friend I was so sorry this had happened to her, and I asked her how she was feeling. She said she felt surprised that she was dead, but then she felt equally surprised to find herself in this place of the afterlife that did not resemble anything she had been taught to expect. She described the place—a kind of communications facility equipped with devices such as the one she was using to communicate with me right now. She said she had been asked to help out with experiments being conducted to improve communication between the spirit realm and the people still living on Earth, and she had chosen me for her experiment, which is why she was speaking with me now.

I felt concerned for my friend, and I asked her if she felt safe and okay, and she said, "Oh, yeah, I'm fine. This is an interesting place. I don't mind being here. I'm just still a little shocked by all of this, but I'm not in any pain, and everyone here has been friendly."

I wanted to learn more from my friend, but our communication seemed to fizzle out like a phone that gets disconnected, and I woke up. I told my husband, Demitri, about this dream, and he suggested we go to a restaurant that had been owned by mutual friends and who might have heard something about our friend's death as well. The moment we entered the restaurant, our mutual friends rushed to us to tell us about our friend's tragic fate. They described how she had died in the very same details that she had given me in the dream. I asked them how they learned of our friend's death, and they said that her family had called to let them know. I told them about my dream, and their jaws dropped. I said, "Maybe that's why I had the dream—to let you know she's okay."

But, that was not the last time I heard from my friend. Several months later, Demitri and I stopped at another restaurant that had once been owned by our friend and her husband. After she died, her husband sold the restaurant to start a new life in another state. We wondered about the new management and how the restaurant might have changed. After we ordered our meals, I went to the restroom. As I was washing my hands, I looked in the mirror, and there she stood, directly behind me. She studied me intensely as though she wanted to be certain that I had seen her. She said nothing. I was not afraid of her presence because I knew her. She had a heart of gold, and she would never want to harm me or anyone, under any circumstance. I turned around to speak with her, and she disappeared.

I felt disappointed and frustrated. Did I miss something she had wanted to tell me? Why did she leave without speaking? What was she expecting from me? Was there something she wanted me to do for her? I worried that I may have disappointed her because I wasn't understanding something she may have needed me to understand.

A couple of months later, I heard from my friend again, this time through telepathy. Her family had asked Demitri and me to help them with her belongings, and I was assigned the task of driving her car to a new location. The moment I turned on the car, a tape of Cat Stevens' song, "Wild World" began to play. I felt my friend's energy, but it seemed to come from a time she had experienced in the past. I could feel everything she had felt, and I knew that on that day she had been driving aimlessly, anywhere, just to get away. I felt her stress, anger, and sadness. I knew she had just been in a fight with her husband, and she felt crushed and alone. I felt all her anguish and cried her tears. I was experiencing her story as she had lived it in that moment. I should mention, this was not the car she had been killed in. That event had occurred later in her life and in a different car.

As soon as I exited the car, I no longer felt my friend's energy, but I also did not feel any more enlightened by this communication with her than I had before. Once again, I did not know why she communicated with me or what she had actually wanted me to know or do. All I could do was pray for her and ask the divine universal energy to comfort her and help her to feel loved and happy wherever she was now. I did not tell her family about any of this. This information could not have helped them with their grief. I told only Demitri, and he agreed this was not useful or helpful information for anyone who knew our friend.

After that event, I never heard from my friend again. The only reason she had ever given for contacting me had been that she was conducting a communication experiment. Perhaps that is all there was to it. The first mode of communication had been her talking with me in a dream. The second mode of communication was visual. She appeared to me when I was wide awake and in a place she had once worked. The third and final mode of communication was through telepathy or what some might call channeling, and this time in a car she had driven. Apparently, three experiments had been conducted, and I was simply at the receiving end. Because I have no other explanation, I have to accept my friend satisfied the requirements of the experiments. She did successfully make contact with me in three different ways. There might not have been any other message that had to be communicated, at least not to me. Maybe nothing more had been expected of me. I have to trust that if something else was needed from me, my friend would have been able to deliver the message.

I was happy to have been of help to my friend in any way I could. I suppose if I had refused to communicate with her, she would not have been able to conduct her communication experiments with me, but refusing did not occur to me. I was eager to help and to learn whatever she wanted me to learn.

So, what did I learn from these strange divine interventions? Well, I learned there are many possible realities to which our souls might travel after this life, just as there are many different places one can go when living here on Earth. I learned that we might actually be asked to do work in these afterlife realities, just as my friend had been asked to partake in experiments that would improve communication between the souls living there in the purely spiritual realm and those who are still here on Earth in the material realm. In the process, I learned that, apparently, the divine universal energy wants to bridge the communication gap between these worlds.

Finally, I learned that paranormal phenomena or divine intervention is real. The confirmation from others of every detail my friend had told me about her death in a dream gave me undeniable evidence that our souls' lives continue after we depart from this world, and we can, in fact, communicate with those who still live here on Earth, and in more than one way.

This experience begs the question, why does the divine universal energy that exists in the purely spiritual realm want to communicate with us here on Earth? The most logical answer is to make the unknown known, but, again, why?

To answer that question, I must take an inventory of the effect of this knowledge on me. I can tell you it has always comforted me. Even when I sometimes feel confused by these paranormal experiences, I find it comforting to know that there is no finality in death. My loved ones who have traveled to the spirit realm are still alive there, and it is even possible for me to connect with them before I depart from this world. Our relationships do not need to end. We can still share the energy of thoughts and feelings no matter where we are.

Knowledge of divine intervention is knowledge of everlasting life. In addition to my experience with my friend, I have experienced several contacts with other loved ones who have departed from this world, and, so far, I have found them all to be happy and well cared for.

There have been times when I seem to travel to the spiritual realm in my dreams. I have visited with one of my grandmothers in her new reality. She was sitting in a comfortable chair, surrounded by bright white light, smiling radiantly. I don't recall what we spoke about, but her joy was unmistakable, and I believe she was merely letting me know all is well, and death is not to be feared.

I have visited family members getting ready for Easter dinner in their spirit world. They were gathered in a kitchen that looked just like any kitchen on Earth, and, again, the light was brilliant. Everyone was happier than I had ever seen them to be in this world. During this occasion, I saw my biological mother sitting at a table while her mother was happily preparing dinner. My mother was listening to someone who seemed to be her spiritual mentor or counselor. She was intensely focused on this conversation, and she did not notice my presence. I was not able to see the spirit who was talking with her, but I could see my mother's face, hair, and clothing in every detail. I even touched her hair. Still, she did not notice my presence. I felt her keen interest in every word being spoken to her, but I could not see the speaker, and I could not hear what the speaker was saying. Clearly, though, from my mother's intense focus, I could discern this was no ordinary conversation. My mother was learning something extremely important to her. I felt that her spiritual mentor was giving her instructions for her next mission, and she really wanted to be sure she would remember. She had tuned out all distractions.

Though every spirit with whom I have visited in the afterlife seems to be living in a different place or a different context, the one thing their spiritual realities have in common during the moments of my visits is they reflect some familiar aspect of this material world on Earth, and all the souls living within these contexts are happy. In addition, all the spirits with whom I have visited appear to have guidance from other souls who are more advanced in their spiritual growth. They might be angels or they might be spirit teachers, but whoever they are, I feel assured they have nothing but good intentions. From the joyfulness of my loved ones, I sense that they are surrounded by divine, unconditional love, no matter where their spiritual journeys have taken them.

I have come to the conclusion, the mentors, guides, and angels in the purely spiritual realm wish to communicate with us in this material realm because they want to help us. They want us to know there is nothing to fear in this life or the next, and if we want their help and guidance, all we need to do is ask for it. They will answer, lovingly, and without judgement. They want us to know we don't have to die to be near God. All we need to do is have faith and pray or meditate.

Imagine living without fear, knowing that no matter what, whether you live here or depart from this Earth to live somewhere else, you and your loved ones will be okay. How much freer would you be to love, live, create, and be happy? When the unknown becomes known, we can be assured super-natural love is real, in whatever form it takes. In addition, this love is always available to us—to heal us, guide us, and protect us.

We are merely spirits living in a material world for now, but as our journey continues, we are bound for other worlds and other adventures, and throughout it all, we will be loved. We will never be abandoned by the divine universal energy. How much better is life, knowing we have friends in this life and the next who will help us through it all?

The key thing to remember, however, is we have free will. Even God will not help us if we refuse to ask for it and receive it. We must choose, and to be able to make that choice, we need to trust the divine universal energy. We must believe in its good and loving intentions and interventions. We have to open our minds and hearts to divine intervention before we can experience it. But, once we know without a doubt how much we are loved, we grow, leaps and bounds, day after day. The more we learn and trust, the happier we feel, and, eventually, we find the light known to Heaven, living within us, no matter where we are —here, there, and anywhere.

CHAPTER 8

RELEASING LIMITING BELIEFS

I was 12 years old when the first man walked on the moon on July 20, 1969. Even though we watched this momentous event on TV, I still have troubles believing it actually happened. In 1969 our technology was limited to black and white TV, landline phones, and typewriters. We didn't have cell phones. We didn't have digital cameras. We didn't have email. The internet didn't exist, and the vast majority of Americans had not seen or touched a computer until the early 1980s. Given that our technology was primitive by today's standards, it was easier for me to believe that the media had intentionally deceived us by staging this event somewhere in a desert than it was to believe a man had actually bounced around on the surface of the moon and planted an American flag on it. In my mind, this was science fiction, like something out of a *Star Trek* TV show. It could not be real.

If this same event happened today within the context of today's technology, I would find it easier to believe. However, even today, like many Americans, I do not trust the "news." Actually, I trust it less now than ever before because the "news" is overtly lying to us, so overtly it doesn't even match up to any semblance of common sense. It is more obviously nonsense. Rarely is there any authentic investigative journalism. Most "news" stories are yellow journalism, that is, propaganda with a political agenda. Americans have been lied to so much that even when there is an abundance of evidence, we are reluctant to trust anything we read or hear on the "news," which is the main reason, I think, many people deny the reality of global warming, despite all the scientific evidence. If you don't live in the Arctic where you can actually see the rapid melting of ice or feel the abnormal increase in temperature, it is difficult to believe global warming is real, especially when the climate hasn't seemed to change that much, if at all, where you live.

When it comes to discerning whether something is true, experience or the lack of experience can play a big part in our judgement calls. The more skeptical we are, the more difficult it is to believe that anything we have not personally experienced is real. We are more likely to believe that the storyteller is a liar or maybe crazy. Anything outside our personal experience can seem too bizarre to be credible. This is understandable. The only way we can be sure something is possible is if we have had a similar experience to the story we are being told. How can we expect anyone to believe in the impossible? To do so requires an extraordinary imagination or gullibility.

On the other hand, if you have had many bizarre and inexplicable experiences, you might come to see life as surreal, like theater of the absurd, and you could be more open to the idea that anything is possible. Francis Bacon had said, "They are ill discoverers that think there is no land when they see nothing but sea." Indeed, the more experiences we have, the more we are likely to be open to new possibilities, while others who have had less experiences will be inclined to believe in impossibilities. If we have seen nothing but sea, we will likely not be able to believe in the possibility of the existence of land because there would be no schema in our brains for it. And for the same reason, if we have seen nothing but land, we are likely to disbelieve in the possibility of the sea. However, if we have seen both the sea and the land, and add to that, we have seen more than a few strange and inexplicable creatures residing in the sea and on the land, we will not readily dismiss stories of such possibilities. Rather, we will be more likely to be curious, and our curiosity will motivate us to make our own inquiries and explorations to discover whether the alleged impossible could actually be possible.

I have found both atheists and religious people have this limitation in their world views in common. Both have blinders to new possibilities. Atheists tend to never question the authority of science while religious people tend to never question the authorities of their religions. Interestingly, both parties tend to close themselves off from experiencing the mysterious. They limit their experiences to the dogma of their respective authorities. Just as interestingly, they limit their discussion of the concept of the Divine as a God who is likened to an old man with a beard living somewhere in the heavens who is controlling everyone and everything. Neither party seems able to conceive of the possibility of the Divine as something that is not tangible and not external to us. Neither party is open to introspection or to the mystery of life that cannot be measured or absolutely explained.

To their credit, however, quantum physicists are beginning to explore the realms of the alleged impossible, and, in the process, they are coming to the same understanding of many ancient philosophers that there is something more to life than mere tangible objects, and we have something more to do with the manifestation of our own realities than we might have believed before. Quantum physicists are beginning to understand what ancient philosophers had tried to explain--how our thoughts and beliefs have more than just a little influence on the creation of our own experiences, including our physical realities. Rather than dismiss philosophers like Descartes who said, "I think, therefore I am," Quantum Physicists are beginning to discover the ancient philosophers were not just speculating or wildly dreaming up their ideas. Rather, they were trying to explain their experiences, which were real to them. They just did not have the means to prove their experiences with the factual evidence that one might gather from a science lab.

I can only speak for myself, and because I have had wild and inexplicable experiences, I tend to be more open to the idea that what might be considered impossible could be possible, maybe even critical to our ability to survive and thrive. I have learned that releasing limiting beliefs that do not serve our highest good is a practice that should be embraced because opening our minds to new possibilities can enhance the quality of our lives, especially the beliefs about ourselves that limit our experiences and can cause us to be stuck in situations or relationships that are harmful to us. If I believed, for example, that I am helpless, I will do nothing to improve my life. On the other hand, if I believe I have the inner resources and strength to change my life, including obtaining help when I need it, I am more likely to make changes that have positive outcomes. Both my clients and I have experienced these positive outcomes.

To release limiting beliefs, we must first make the decision that there could be more to life than just our own experiences, and we must be willing to explore the experiences we have had with an open mind, questioning whether what we experienced is real or merely imagined and whether our experiences have taught us something useful or beneficial. We must make a deliberate effort to exercise our imagination to visualize new possibilities and be willing to question our assumptions and beliefs as well as question those whom we have deemed as the ultimate authorities, albeit our parents, scientists, or religious authorities. Finally, we must be willing to experiment in our daily lives, making different choices based on the new beliefs we are testing to gather our own evidence as to whether these new beliefs serve us in making our lives happier or in achieving our goals.

To keep an open mind, I find it useful to reflect on a paradoxical statement made by Thomas Henry Huxley in 1886, "I am too much of a skeptic to deny the possibility of anything." And so, I am willing to believe that maybe, just maybe, a man really did walk on the moon in 1969, despite my lack of experience with such technology. It also helps to have a cousin who is literally a rocket scientist. She is an honest person, so I will give her the benefit of my doubt.

CHAPTER 9

LOGIC AND INSIGHT

The best epiphanies I have experienced are those that begin with a question to which I seek an answer through employing both logic and insight. Logic is a scientific way of thinking, based on observations of phenomena that can be easily repeated or duplicated and are therefore regarded as facts. These facts are used as premises for an argument that ends with a deduction or logical conclusion. Logic is demonstrated in mathematical equations and in persuasive writing in the same way. They both express, "If this is true, then something else must also be true." For example, if it is true that there is gravity, then it must also be true that anything that goes up must come down. One could say there is something like a mirror in logical thinking. In my example, gravity became a fact as a result of repeated observation of objects falling to the ground. If we regard gravity as a true law of nature on Earth, then we must logically conclude that no matter what object we might throw into the air, it will fall down. Knowing this fact will deter most of us from jumping off tall buildings, which prevents us from experiencing great harm. Clearly, logic is essential to our survival.

Insight is derived from an internal extra sense that might be called intuition or inspiration. The word denotes its meaning. It literally means to see inside. To have insight is to possess knowledge and understanding that is derived from our own internal processes that involve introspection and sometimes divine inspiration that has come to us out of the blue, perhaps in a dream.

In addition to being a renowned scientist, Albert Einstein was a profound philosopher whose insights will be remembered for centuries to come. He was keenly in tune with his internal processes that gave him insight. For example, he had said that he had a dream about the theory of relativity. He then later used math, i.e., logic, to prove the theory. The theory had come from inspiration or that extra sense, not from facts or observed phenomena. Einstein had been known to excuse himself from dinner parties to commune with his internal muses who he said had been calling him. Einstein had great respect for intuition as a source of information. He stated, "The intuitive mind is a sacred gift, and the rational mind is a faithful servant."

Perhaps Einstein's genius had come from his extraordinary openness to information, regardless of its source. Rather than close his mind to the possibility of other-worldly sources of knowledge outside the usual realm of science, he chose to keep an open mind, which empowered him to hear the inner voices of invisible muses who were willing to work with him. Perhaps genius is merely the result of a curious and open mind that does not allow biases to block information that might be helpful, regardless of its source.

I am no Einstein. However, I have had similar experiences with combining insight with logic. The best example I can provide is a time when I was in graduate school working on a literary analysis paper on Herman Melville's novel, *Pierre*, for an American Literature class. Our professor had instructed us to select a work of literature for our thesis, and get his approval of our selection before we began our research. When I requested permission to write my thesis on *Pierre*, the professor laughed and shook his head. "Absolutely NOT," he said. I asked him why. He answered, "Okay, I will tell you why. You see, many of the best literary critics have tried to understand that book and failed. One of them even died trying because he made a vow he would not eat until he had figured it out. He actually starved to death."

"What?" I said. "That's crazy!"

"Yes, it is," he responded. "But that really happened. That book drives everyone crazy. So, please don't do it."

I had to make a deal with my professor. I told him his story made me even more intrigued, and I could not resist the challenge to try to understand *Pierre*. I assured him that I believed I had a chance of at least offering a little more insight to the conversation among the literary critics because I loved Melville. After all, I was one of the few who picked up on his dark sense of humor in *Moby Dick*. I promised the professor I would not starve myself to death, and if I felt like I was becoming too obsessed or losing my mind, I would stop.

He said, "Well, obviously, I can't stop you. But you must be true to your promise! The minute you feel like you are losing it, you must stop! If necessary, I will give you an extension to work on something else."

We sealed the deal, and I nearly ran to the library to collect all the books and articles I could find on *Pierre*, Melville, the history and culture of his time, and his literary contemporaries. I was on a treasure hunt, determined to find all the clues and the ultimate key to the meaning of *Pierre*. I read everything I had found in the library, taking copious notes on the main points. I pondered the same questions other literary critics had posed, such as why did Melville write in old language, using words like "Thee" and "Thou" in the dialogs? This novel seemed to have nothing in common with his other works. Yet, there was something they must have had in common, but what? Certainly the idea of chasing after the truth was a theme in *Moby Dick* as well. But what was the point in *Pierre*?

One night as I was sitting at my typewriter, and, yes, this was before word processing, I was deep in thought, pouring over all my notes, pondering these questions. I paused and looked out the window. I saw my own reflection in the dim light from my desk, and I almost jumped out of my chair, frightened by my image. I looked like an old man with a severely stern face. I never saw myself in that light before. Others had told me I looked very angry at times, but I had not been feeling angry at all. I had just been deep in thought. Now I got a glimpse at what they saw on my face, and it frightened me. I thought, "Oh, man, if I look like that, no wonder, they think I'm angry!"

I realized *Pierre* was starting to drive me crazy, but I wasn't willing to give up just yet. Instead, I decided to go to bed, hoping some rest might help me to have clarity in the morning. I had a long dream that night. In the dream, a man spoke to me, lecturing like a professor. Throughout, I nodded my head and said, "aha, aha." At the end of the lecture, I woke up. All I could remember from the entire lecture were the words, "hero fantasy." I mulled it over for a few minutes, and, suddenly, I knew the answer.

I jumped out of bed and furiously typed my paper. I knew, I just KNEW, Melville's *Pierre* was a satire with the sole intention to poke fun at his fellow authors of his time. In fact, ALL his works were targeting them, including *Moby Dick*, and his novella, *Billy Budd*. Melville detested the optimism and romanticism of men like Ralph Waldo Emerson and Henry Davis Thoreau. He believed they saw the world through rose-colored glasses, denying the reality of the suffering that was his life and the life of most people. Indeed, all of Melville's "heroes" were laughable, self-deluded men who believed they knew the Truth with a capital T, only to discover in the end they knew nothing, and their lives ended tragically, due to their own ignorance of reality. The reason for the elevated old language in *Pierre* was to heighten the sense of self-deluded importance of the protagonist. Pierre, like the authors of the Bible, believed he and only he knew the Truth. His wealthy father had warned him not to marry his girlfriend.

However, Pierre insisted on marrying her anyway, assuming that his wealthy father was prejudiced against his girlfriend because she was poor. When he married the love of his life, his father disowned him, and Pierre lost all financial assistance and the possibility of inheriting his father's wealth. Pierre and his wife lived in hardship as a result, but Pierre was sure of his calling to fight for the Truth. By a stroke of twisted fate at the end of the story, Pierre learns the actual truth. He had married his half-sister, his father's secret baby conceived with his mistress during an extramarital affair. Upon learning this, Pierre cannot live with himself, and he commits suicide.

Pierre was Melville's ultimate warning to the American Renaissance authors of the danger of their rose-colored glasses. The mid-20th century literary critics were trying to understand the novel from within the context of their own time. They didn't understand it from Melville's point of view because he was speaking mostly to his peers. In fact, most literary critics never understood Melville's dark humor in his other works either, so they didn't figure out that *Pierre* was a satire, a parody of men who are bloated with self-importance, heroes only in their own minds.

My professor expressed his astonishment at my insight when he read my paper. He said, "My God! I believe you found the real meaning! You are the only one who figured this out! How did you do it?"

I couldn't tell my professor what he would not believe, but I must say now, I had help. I believe to this day, Herman Melville himself spoke to me in my dream. He was the teacher in my dream lecturing to me. I have to assume Melville wanted his work to be understood, and I was receptive to hearing from his spirit. He gave me the insight, and then I proved it with logic, just as Einstein had a dream about the theory of relativity and then used logic to prove it.

I may have been receptive, and Melville's spirit may have wanted to communicate with me because I felt love for the man, even though he had lived far before my time. I felt he was a kindred spirit. Ironically, I felt the same love for Emerson and Thoreau. I understood both sides, the optimism and the cynicism.

To this day I feel a kinship with all these authors. I understand life is hard, but I also understand there is some heaven in it too. I like to focus on the heavenly consolation to cope with the hardships, but, man, I do get it. Sometimes we have to choose between laughing or crying, which is why I understand Melville's dark humor. Something tells me he did not hate his optimistic and romantic peers. In fact, I think he wished he could have found a pair of rose-colored glasses for himself too.

The greatest lesson I learned from the *Pierre* epiphany is that the best answers come from the marriage of logic and insight, and your mind must remain open to both. You never know where you might find an answer. It could come from a book or an experiment in a science lab. Or, it could come from the man next door, a child, a movie, a song, and maybe even a spirit or an angel who speaks to you in your dreams.

A friend once said, "I believe we all stumble on the truth every now and then, but most of us choose to ignore it." I have to admit, there's merit in his observation. I know I have ignored my inner voice more than I like to admit, thinking, "That can't be right, I have no logical evidence." I have regretted ignoring my intuition every time. Later, after I have suffered the consequences, I think, "Holy cow! I should have listened to my intuition! It was right!"

Most of the time, intuition comes before logic, which is one reason many of us choose to ignore it. We live in a culture that teaches us we must have scientific evidence to accept something as true. However, I have learned to listen to my inner voice, and not wait for logic to kick in. I know now I can trust my inner voice. Eventually, the whole story will be revealed, and logical evidence will come, but waiting for it could be a big mistake. Many times, my quiet inner voice has steered me away from what would have led to harmful, even fatal, outcomes. Experience has taught me I would be a fool to ignore it.

That said, I believe logic must not be ignored either. Cognitive dissonance does not serve us; it only leads us to irrational choices that can cause much harm to ourselves or others. Questioning our beliefs and testing them against logic is a healthy practice that can help us to advance in our spiritual evolution every bit as much as being open to our inner processes that can receive help from the great unknown, which cannot be known in any other way but through our own mysterious and inexplicable connection to the divine universal energy.

CHAPTER 10

THE SPIRIT OF ADVENTURE

Where my upbringing lacked in spiritual guidance, it was abundantly blessed in the spirit of adventure. Every weekend and every family vacation was an adventure. During the winter we went downhill skiing. During the spring, summer, and fall, we went canoeing, camping and hiking in the wilderness. One of our favorite adventures was canoeing the Vermillion River in LaSalle County, Illinois, a class II-III Whitewater River. We looked forward to going there every summer to improve our canoeing skills and challenge each other to try to get through the most dangerous part of the river called, the Wild Cat, without tipping over our canoes. I remember the thrill we felt just anticipating the challenge and the fun of hearing our family and friends cheering us on from the river rocks overlooking the Wild Cat. No matter whether we tipped over or stayed afloat, it was still fun. We knew we could count on our fellow canoeists to help us get out from under the whitewater if we ever got in a real bind.

Still, we felt a little trepidation about the possibility of getting trapped under our tipped-over canoes or getting busted up by rocks we didn't manage to avoid. There was only so much other canoeists could do for us. They could pull us out of the water, but for injuries, they could only patch us up with basic first-aid. So much depended on the eyes of the person in the bow and the ears and swift response of the person in the stern. The person in the bow was responsible for spotting on-coming rocks and shouting over the roar of the whitewater, "Rock on the right! Rock on the left! Rock straight ahead!" And the person in the stern of the canoe had to be listening closely and to be able to aggressively and swiftly steer the canoe clear from the rocks. By the time I was a teenager, I had become as good a canoeist as any from these family adventures. It is certainly one way to gain self-confidence, and with proper training and the safety net of others there to help you, it is a good way.

I have since learned that this spirit of adventure I had as a child is beneficial and applicable to everything I do in life. It has served me well in work projects, social interactions, and relationships, and it has helped me to sustain the playfulness and wonderment of my inner child who loves a good challenge and enjoys exploring and learning something new every day. It has helped me to broaden my horizons and discover and develop new strengths. It has also helped me to venture into the unknown intellectually and spiritually, taking on the quest for answers to presumably unanswerable questions. I love a good mystery, not in the sense of a murder mystery, but in the sense of finding clues to the meaning of life, human nature, and the ethereal or paranormal experiences I believe most of us have had but choose to discount or ignore.

My curiosity is insatiable, and it takes me to uncharted territories. I am not satisfied with someone else's answers. I will consider everyone else's perspective and ponder what I feel is noteworthy from a logical and experiential point of view, but I don't just automatically buy into handed-down conventions or beliefs. Not only is it fun to question and put the clues together to come to my own conclusions, it is abundantly rewarding.

When I have tested out an idea or theory with my own daily life experiments and come to that "a-ha" moment, I can then finally form my own conviction that serves me well thereafter. A firm conviction can only be made after much effort and time spent on questioning and testing and putting the clues together to form a logical conclusion that also feels right and matches up to my own discoveries gathered from my own experiments and explorations. When I have formed a solid conviction, I have no need to argue or to convert anyone to my belief. I am simply satisfied to have filled out my own life's map a little more, which gives me more direction and guidance for my life's purpose and how I will choose to live. Every hard-earned conviction I possess gives me additional self-knowledge. I know where I want to be and where I do not want to be. I know what I want and what I don't want. I am more empowered to identify and defend my personal boundaries, and I am more able to achieve my goals. Because my convictions are hard-earned, I need no one's approval or agreement. I am content to know and stand in my own truth and move on to learn something new again.

I do not ever assume I have all the answers, and I encourage everyone to find their own answers. I would never want to know everything. How dull that would be! I look forward to every new mystery, adventure, and exploration. I also enjoy being proven wrong, even after I have formed a conviction, because learning something new is thrilling! It is a splash of whitewater on my face, a flash of lightning, and the rolling drumbeat of thunder. What is life without the adventure of learning?

To live with the wonderment, curiosity, and playfulness of our inner child is to nourish our souls with new life every day. It is to live mindfully in the present moment, seeing it as brand new and completely unique from any moment we have experienced in the past, studying it for the secrets of life itself, and allowing it to teach us something we never knew before, and maybe even something no one has ever known before.

There is nothing to fear in the spirit of adventure. Conversely, fear of leaving our comfort zones or of questioning the handed-down, conventional answers of our cultures can result in the stagnation of our souls, and stagnation leads to a gradual death, like the wilting of a flower that has no fresh water to give it life.

To live is to learn, and to learn is to step out of our comfort zones and take on new challenges, explore new ways of thinking, new possibilities, and new ideas. With the spirit of adventure, it is easy to step out of your comfort zone. In fact, you can look forward to it. You will most likely come out of your adventure feeling more alive.

C HAPTER 11

THE COSMIC PERSPECTIVE

Throughout the ages, theologians, philosophers, poets, and scientists have struggled to reconcile the idea of a benevolent and all-powerful God with the reality of suffering. Perhaps Albert Einstein said it best, "The most important decision we make is whether we believe we live in a friendly or hostile universe."

C.S. Lewis made a noble attempt to explain why God lets us suffer in his book, *The Problem of Pain*. Lewis argues the problem is not that God does not love us; it is that he loves us too much. Lewis sees God as a father figure who occasionally practices tough love to teach us life lessons that compel us to grow stronger in our faith. Per Lewis, God does not want us to suffer, but, sometimes suffering is the only way we learn, like some children who will only learn the hard way, or like the Prodigal Son in Jesus's parable who does not appreciate his father and the life his father had provided him until after he had left home and made many bad choices that left him alone and desolate. Completely humbled and desperate, the Prodigal Son returns to his father and asks for forgiveness. In response, his father celebrates his return.

Before Lewis, many theologians debated the idea of predestination versus free will. Some believed we have no control over our fate, and we merely need to learn to accept our lot in life. Others believed our own free will is the sole cause of our suffering, and to blame God is to shirk responsibility for our poor choices and bad behaviors.

Hindu theologians discussed karma, the idea that whatever we do comes back to us like a boomerang. If we mistreat others, we will at some point experience the same maltreatment, and if we treat others well, we will experience the same generosity and kindness we had given. Jesus mentions the same idea—we reap what we sow.

Both Hindu teachers and ancient Greek philosophers, including Socrates and his student, Plato, believed in reincarnation, the idea that our souls don't just disappear into the ether of a heavenly place. Instead, they return to the Earth in new bodies with a new or renewed purpose to learn, to teach, and to experience whatever our souls need to increase our wisdom or to free ourselves from karmic debts.

Many of today's theologians are discussing spiritual laws in terms of quantum physics, popularizing the idea that we manifest our own realities through the Law of Attraction. According to this theory, our thoughts, beliefs, and emotions create our experiences, both good and bad. In essence, their warning is the old adage, "Be careful what you wish for, you might get it." However, they add the idea that we should also be careful of what we fear, because our focus on what we fear will bring that exactly into our experience. The Law of Attraction is amoral. It makes no judgement. It simply responds to our every thought, good or bad, indiscriminately.

The downside to the Law of Attraction is we might not always be aware of our thoughts or in control of them. Not only do we have an average of sixty thousand thoughts per day, we also have both a conscious and a subconscious mind. Few of us would consciously choose to have experiences that cause us suffering. So, if we are manifesting painful experiences, we must be doing it subconsciously. Also, it does not take into account children or others whose cognitive development is limited. In addition, it begs the question of how much others' thoughts, beliefs, and feelings are imposed upon us or cause our experiences. In a battle of wills, which one of us wins? For example, I certainly do not wish to be attacked, yet, someone else might wish to attack me. Whose wish will determine the experience?

The question of how much control we have in determining our life experiences has been with us since the beginning of human existence. Ancient mythology from every culture depicts all-powerful gods and goddesses to whom humans are merely their play things that they mercilessly toss around for their entertainment, lust, or revenge. In this ancient paradigm, humans have absolutely no control over their lives. They can only hope that some god or goddess will be in a good mood and smile in their direction. This idea of gods and goddesses brings to mind the historian, Lord Acton, who wrote, "Power tends to corrupt, and absolute power corrupts absolutely. Great men are almost always bad men." It seems to me the idea of an all-powerful and indifferent god is also a bad god, especially if this god is a self-worshipping and jealous god whose only aim is to show off his power and force the powerless to obey his every random command.

Perhaps the question of who or what is to blame for our experiences does not serve us. Perhaps what matters most is what we do with our own power, whether we use it to serve our own and others' highest good, or whether we use it to harm. In regard to the idea of God, maybe the best questions are whether God is loving or indifferent, helpful or harmful, a random tyrant or a wise counselor. Also, perhaps this God is not all-powerful, which would be the case if we have our own power of free will. And perhaps, God is not one persona. Perhaps God is in all of us and expressed in many different ways.

The only God that makes sense to me is a type of energy that is made only of pure love and that manifests healing, joy, wisdom, and beauty. This God is a power available to us all if we choose to accept it. When power is used to harm, this is not God. It is an opposite energy that is made of pure disdain for others and worships itself. This type of power or energy is also available to all of us if we choose it, and it is called evil.

Perhaps the only control we have is the choice of which power or energy we will accept and strengthen within ourselves, and which energy will we call upon for help. Perhaps this choice determines how we respond to our experiences, whether or not we have caused them to happen, and this choice will influence our future experiences, for better or worse.

The intention to love will likely manifest joyful experiences. Conversely, the intention to hate will likely manifest painful experiences. Maybe the cosmic perspective is really just this simple.

CHAPTER 12

NAMASTE

The Eastern Indian greeting of Namaste has become popular in the West. I first encountered it at the end of a yoga class. The instructor explained the word had its roots in the ancient Sanskrit word meaning "to bow down to you". The Namaste greeting involves pressing both palms of your hands together, placing them on your heart, and slightly bowing your head as you speak, "Namaste." Our yoga instructor further explained that the whole of the gesture means more than just bowing. It is a way to express, "The Divine in me honors the Divine in you."

To be greeted in such a way is to feel at once humbled and honored. Just thinking about the intention and meaning of Namaste touches me in the same way as a heart-felt prayer. I find it to be a beautiful reminder that we all carry within us a divine spark. To greet people in this manner is to reveal your intention to connect with them on a deeply spiritual level, soul to soul. Namaste elevates us and humbles us at the same time because we are reminded we both have the divine within us, and neither of us is superior or inferior to the other.

I have learned since that some of the ancient Eastern Indian religions teach that each of us is the one and only God who through creation is exploring the many aspects and possibilities of its nature. According to this teaching, to see ourselves as separate from each other is to forget our divine identity. It is to forget that we are God who is experiencing life in our current forms that may appear separate but are actually expressions of the same God. Perhaps the best analogy is the actor who enjoys playing different characters in different plays, but he is still the same person, the actor, learning different ways to express ideas and telling different stories. In the process of playing the different roles, sometimes the hero, other times the villain or the comical character, the actor learns a great deal about his own different dimensions in his personality and what he likes or dislikes and what he might want to change about himself or how he might make improvements in his creations.

For many Westerners, I imagine this is a mind-blowing concept, especially for those who believe the opposite—that we are all sinners, and God is an external father figure who punishes those who are bad and rewards those who are good. To believe we are actually all the same God playing different roles, one must come to the conclusion that the idea of good and evil is false. According to this idea, there are no real good guys or bad guys, no heroes or villains, no saints, and no devils. There is only God, and we are all God merely experimenting with different personas and expressing ourselves in a variety of forms through our creations.

How would the idea that we are all the same God be experienced in this world? I suppose the God in me must be in agreement with the same God in you to act out whatever roles we are playing together on our shared life stage. Perhaps Shakespeare was more insightful than even he understood when he wrote, "All the world's a stage, and all the men and women merely players."

The only problem with accepting this belief, it seems to me, is although our characters may not be real on this life stage, the pain we suffer when we are injured or ill feels very real. Are we a God who sometimes chooses to experience this pain? Jesus, who, as the story goes, could have called upon an army of angels to rescue him from capture, chose instead to allow himself to suffer crucifixion. The early saints and apostles chose to suffer too. Like Socrates, they would not surrender their convictions to save their lives and chose to allow their enemies to torture and murder them. So, are we a God who bears the cross of the sufferer and at the same time plays the role of the tyrant who tortures himself?

How could this be? Why would anyone choose to suffer? And what about the children? It cannot be right thinking to assume they would choose to suffer. But, what if children are God as much as adults? It is mind boggling just to consider this.

In his book, *Journey of Souls: Case Studies of Lives Between Lives*, Michael Newton, explores the possibility that when we exist as pure energy in the afterlife, we plan out our next life with the help of other souls who are wise counselors. We predestine ourselves, and, sometimes, for the sake of growing stronger and wiser, or for the sake of helping other souls to advance in their spiritual growth, some of us freely choose to suffer in the next life, in essence, to play the role of the victim, child or adult, for the ultimate benefit of improving our own or another's understanding of our divine self. Maybe the one who chooses to suffer needs to learn about the importance of compassion, for example. Or maybe the one who chooses to be the brutal tyrant needs to learn that to live by the sword is to die by the sword. Maybe those who choose to be excessively wealthy need to learn that money really does not buy happiness, and so on.

Though Newton does not explicitly explore the idea that we are all the same God in this book, he does explore the idea that we each have a divine soul within us that is learning and growing from many lifetimes of experience and freely choosing to do so, even at the price of enduring great pain in the process. To accept Newton's view, one must first accept the premise of reincarnation.

Regardless, I find it comforting to believe that we all have at least a part of the divine and loving universal energy within us, despite the many roles we might play on this Earth stage. I also like to believe that the more we see this divine spark within ourselves and others, and the more we make the effort to live soul-to-soul, as opposed to ego-to-ego, the happier we will ultimately be. Personally, I cannot imagine myself choosing to suffer. Indeed, I choose every day to make an effort to be happy and to help others to reduce their suffering. However, I acknowledge there have been many more advanced and greater souls than mine who, for the greater good, had chosen to suffer, and I don't mind saying they are most likely much closer to God than I.

CHAPTER 13

MANY LIVES

I became interested in reincarnation because I had experienced what I would call "flashbacks" in many dreams of what seemed to be memories of previous lives I had experienced. As a child, I had a dream of having been a little girl living in a small early American settlement. In the moment of the dream, I heard drums beating in the distance, which aroused panic. I felt certain we were about to be attacked by American Indians, and I feared, not for my own life, but for my mother's. I ran around the settlement yelling for my mother, but I couldn't find her anywhere, and I woke up in a cold sweat. I cannot remember whether I had this dream before or after my mother had died in this life, but regardless, the experience felt like a memory.

In another childhood dream, I was living in a big city in a more contemporary time. I had never been to a city before having this dream, but when my family took me to Chicago in this life for the first time, it felt strangely familiar as though I had been there before.

As an adult, I have had several more dreams of what seemed to be previous lives. These dreams were much more involved. In one dream, I had been a male violin player in Russia who had frequently performed for Czar Nicholas and his family. As I was walking through the streets one evening, a mob of armed rebels flooded the streets. I was suddenly surrounded by them. One shouted at me, "Take up arms!" I was shocked and confused.

I asked, "Why should I take up arms? What is happening? Why are you doing this?"

A rebel answered, "To overthrow the Czar, of course!"

"But why would I do this? I have nothing against him. I am not political!" I shouted back.

After that, the dream story moved to a different moment. I was among a large group of people being herded into a palace by armed rebels. Again, I was confused. How did I become anyone's enemy? I was not involved in politics. I looked around me and saw that the others in the group were people just like me, ordinary citizens, but some I had recognized as fellow musicians or scholars, and one was a dear friend of mine. None of us understood why we had been targeted by these rebels. We did not see ourselves as anyone's enemy. We had no power and no money.

The rebels forced us to climb a large, winding staircase in the palace. When I reached nearly the top of the staircase, I looked down and saw other rebels vandalizing the main floor. When I saw them chopping away and destroying the grand piano, I felt my heart break, and I cried out, "No, please! Stop! Please! Don't destroy the music of Mother Russia!" I was ignored. No one heard me above the roar of the riot, and no one cared. Clearly, I was out of step with his moment in Russian history—out of step and clueless, still having no idea why all this was happening. I had spent my life caring only about music, and I had been oblivious to everything else.

Once the group reached the top of the stairs, we were forced into a room where we were herded onto bleachers that had been used for choir performances. My dear friend and I held hands as we looked out at the rebels standing on the floor in front of us lifting their rifles. There were only a few of them, and I realized that they would not be able to shoot all of us at the same time, and we would be forced to watch each other die slowly. I shouted down to the rebels, "If you are going to kill us, please get some more guns in here so we can all die together! You don't have enough guns!" Again, I was ignored. My friend squeezed my hand as we watched the rebels raise their rifles at us, and suddenly the reality of what was happening to us registered, and my last thought was, "Oh my, God! This is a holocaust!"

In that moment, an inner voice spoke to me, "You don't need to see the rest," and I woke up, returned to this life.

When I had this dream, I knew nothing of Russian history, but because this dream had been so vivid in all its details, I became curious to see if it in any way had reflected some part of Russian history. The dream gave me a lot of clues for pinning down the time. This was obviously the end of the reign of Czar Nicholas, and the rebels had to be the ones who had overthrown him. These clues led me to researching the history, and I concluded my murderers in that dream scenario had to have been in association with Vladimir Lenin. More research on Lenin revealed he had in fact killed off many innocent Russian citizens, especially as he grew increasingly powerful and paranoid. Several years later, the Chicago Tribune published an article on the history of the Winter Palace in Russia, and I was stunned to see the exact staircase that I had climbed in the dream just before I had been executed. I could see the very place I had stood when I pleaded with the rebels to stop destroying the music of Mother Russia.

I have mulled over this dream for many years, trying to ascertain why I had it. If it had been in fact a memory of a previous life, why did I revisit this memory? What was the message or the lesson? Obviously the story told is one of a musician who had no interest in politics yet was swept up in it anyway and murdered. Was the dream telling me that there is no escaping politics or the moment of history in which we are born? Was it telling me I should have been more aware of current affairs? Was it telling me that I should be more politically active in this life? I have often thought about what this violin player would have done had he been forewarned of this potential fate. Given that he had no use for politics, he probably would have tried to find a way to protect himself and his friends from it. Would he have been able to? Would awareness of this sudden regime change have made any difference?

Or, maybe I was simply meant to understand that no matter where we live in any lifetime, those who are in power are not to be trusted, no matter what they claim to be their ideology. Lenin, for example, claimed to be following Marxist ideology, but, now having read Marx, it is clear Lenin was nothing more than another violent dictator of whom Marx would never have approved. Marx clearly states economic equality would eventually come about by necessity, not by violence. Marx believed that humankind would at some time in the far away future become collectively enlightened and would willingly choose to distribute wealth and power more fairly for everyone's mutual benefit. He did not intend to start a violent revolution that resulted in the mere replacement of one dictator with another. Rather, Marx's philosophy supports social democracies like what we now see in the Nordic countries where the ordinary citizens are collectively self-governing and freely choosing to share the wealth and power among them, which, as Marx predicted, has resulted in a much higher and more satisfactory quality of life for all the citizens. These Nordic nations today consistently rank at the top of the charts for being the happiest and healthiest people on the planet.

I have had several other vivid dreams that seem to be memories of previous lives. In one dream, I found myself in the shoes of Hitler's niece, someone I had not ever heard of before this dream. In the dream I was a student at a university in Germany. In one moment, I was shocked to learn that a fellow student whom I had believed to be exceptionally intelligent, had been reading the book, *Mein Kampf*. I could not believe anyone with a brain could in any way take this book seriously. It was so irrational and illogical. In another part of the dream, I was sitting in Hitler's apartment balcony watching a parade of Nazi soldiers pass by. I was overcome with fear. I could feel my heart pounding rapidly. I was afraid Hitler would discover I had been secretly working in the underground movement against him.

Research I did on this dream confirmed that Hitler did in fact have a niece who had lived with him in his apartment and who attended a university in Germany. I even found photographs of the apartment balcony where I had been so afraid during the Nazi parade. In fact, Hitler did watch Nazi parades from this balcony. I also learned about the underground movement called the White Rose, which had been a group of college students secretly trying to sabotage the Nazis. However, I could not find any evidence that Hitler's niece had been a member of this movement. All I could find was some literature that read like gossipy fiction that depicted Hitler's niece as a silly young woman who dated Nazi soldiers, which made Hitler, who was said to have been in love with his niece, become jealous. Hitler did in fact murder his niece, but historians don't know why. They merely speculate that he killed her out of a jealous rage because some neighbor heard them quarreling right before they heard the gunshot.

Because of my dream, I believe I could be the only person who knows who Hitler's niece really was and why Hitler killed her. If she had been dating Nazi soldiers, it was most likely her way of spying and getting information to help the White Rose movement. Of course, a dream about a previous life would never hold up as historical facts to anyone else, but I am convinced. After all, I never even knew Hitler had a niece or even that he had lived in an apartment with a balcony where he stood to watch Nazi parades before I had this dream.

I have had many more dreams that I now regard as memories of previous lives. I have been both a white settler and a Native American woman. I have been a Black slave who had a very loving and wise grandfather who even in this life sometimes speaks to me in my dreams to reassure me. I have been a young man who was a member of a revolutionary band of men living somewhere in Latin America who together secretly wired a dictator's mansion with dynamite during a party and ran like hell to get out of there before it exploded. We watched the mansion explode from a nearby ditch. I had this dream repeatedly and in exactly the same detail every time.

Not all the dreams have provided enough clues to enable me to find their exact place and time in history, but the ones that did provide sufficient clues have convinced me that reincarnation is real. I believe I have lived many lives, maybe even more than I can remember in this life. The idea of reincarnation has been with every age of humankind, in the ancient East and the ancient West. Even Plato discussed it, and he spoke of the River of Forgetfulness from which all souls are commanded to drink before they are incarnated into this world again. Plato acknowledged that some people do remember aspects of their previous lives, and it all depends on how much of the River of Forgetfulness they drank. According to Plato, some people may have only taken a sip while others may have taken a big gulp. Those who drank less, remember more of their previous lives.

My exploration of the beliefs about reincarnation has also convinced me that it makes sense. Our souls have so much to learn before we will be sufficiently enlightened to be able to live in harmony with each other for any sustainable amount of time around the globe. What does not make sense is to think we can learn it all in only one lifetime.

CHAPTER 14

REBIRTH

The idea of rebirth is ancient and universal. It exists in some form in every place and culture and in every age of mankind's history. Some view it as synonymous with the idea of transformation like that of a caterpillar transforming into a butterfly, and others view it as reincarnation, which entails a literal, physical death and then a literal rebirth in which the same soul is born again on this Earth into a brand new body. Some view it as being reborn into an afterlife that is not the Earth, but a different place within the universe. Contemporary "born-again Christians" view rebirth differently from the ancient Gnostic Christians. The former believe that to be born again, people must acknowledge they are sinners from birth because they inherited the "original sin" from their fallen ancestors, Adam and Eve, and then they must accept Jesus Christ as their Lord and Savior from sin. The latter, the Gnostic Christians, believed that to be "reborn" was to be reincarnated after a literal death.

Some contemporary psychologists and medical professionals view rebirth as a result of recovering from an illness. With the relief of pain, either emotional or physical, their patients report feeling they are reborn and are able to live more fully. Like the mythological phoenix who rises from the ashes to live again, their patients feel they have risen from adversity. They experience a metaphorical rebirth.

Others view rebirth as a continual process of growing up in the course of natural human development. When we grow from infants to toddlers, our infancy stage of life is forever gone, which can be regarded as a form of death, and as we grow from toddlers to school children, we experience the death of our toddlerhood, and when we grow into adolescents, we experience the death of our early childhood, and as adults, we experience the death of our entire childhood, and so on. With every death of one phase of our human development, a new phase is born. In this way, we are reborn continually throughout a single lifetime. This view of rebirth is similar to transformation like that of a caterpillar who becomes the butterfly, starting life crawling on the ground until it enters its final stage of life with wings to fly. Similarly, as human beings, we begin life crawling, then proceed to walking, then to running, and then to becoming adults who, if all goes well, can take charge of our lives and work toward creating the lives we desire. We might even become self-actualized, that is, Abraham Maslow's idea of the best version of ourselves.

What all the ideas of rebirth have in common is the idea that something must die for something new to live, whether it is a physical or metaphorical death. They all agree that rebirth is a dramatic break from the past. It is the death of an old way of being, which enables a new, and, hopefully better way of being to emerge. The various ideas of rebirth differ only in how and when this process occurs and what its meaning or purpose is.

Those of us who live in places where there are four distinct seasons, spring, summer, fall, and winter, may often think about rebirth upon the arrival of spring when it seems the entire Earth is resurrected from the death-like slumber of winter. Sometimes I wonder if bears feel reborn when they emerge from their long hibernation. The continual cycle of the four seasons seem to remind us of the miracle of birth and rebirth every year, and I cannot see a butterfly without the thought of the miracle of transformation.

During harsh and bitter-cold winter days, I am comforted with the knowledge that spring will come. On dark and rainy spring days with blustering winds, I am comforted with the knowledge of the warmth and bright colors of summer that will come. When summer days are too hot to bear, I am comforted with the knowledge that the crisp, fresh air of fall will come, and on fall days when the trees are bare, and nature loses her color, I am comforted with the knowledge that the beauty of glistening snow will come after gently falling in a peaceful hush from the winter sky.

Just like the four seasons of nature, every season of our lives brings a gift and a challenge. Sometimes the challenge is to choose hope over despair, and, often, the challenge is to allow the past to die so that the present can be fully appreciated, and a brighter future can emerge. Clinging to the past, albeit happy or sad, prevents us from noticing the joy, love, and beauty that is in the Now or that can be created or discovered in the future.

Rebirth might entail the surrender of an unhealthy lifestyle to give birth to a healthy lifestyle. It could also entail allowing a dimension of ourselves to die to allow a more fulfilling dimension to be born. For example, if I have a tendency to be judgmental, and I discover this attitude is not helping me to be a happy person or to have positive relationships, I might choose to work on getting rid of my judgements and biases to make room for a more accepting and welcoming attitude. If I have been too much of a spectator vs. a participant in life, and I discover this has resulted in my feeling detached, disconnected, or lonely, I might choose to move away from the sidelines or stop sitting on the fence and jump into the action.

Any decision we make to change something about ourselves or our lifestyles can lead to a dramatic rebirth. Like the caterpillar, we can discover that we are not condemned to crawl on the ground forever. We can, and, sometimes, we must make dramatic changes that can lead us to a brand new self or self-concept. Our experiences can have the power to change us, and we have the power to change our experiences.

I believe I have experienced rebirth many times within this lifetime, moving from place to place, from one job to another, plus a major career change, getting married and building a family with my husband, replacing old and out-worn beliefs with new beliefs, reassessing my values and priorities, learning to stand up for myself in the least harmful but most effective way, and so on. I have risen from the ashes of adversity more times than I can count, and each time, I have felt born anew--stronger, wiser, happier, and more compassionate, loving, and accepting.

I also believe I have been reincarnated many times, and in each life, as in every season, my soul experienced gifts and challenges. Today, I understand there is a gift in every challenge, perhaps the greatest gift of all. For me, that gift is a stronger sense of the divine within myself and others and a closer bond with the overall divine universal energy, which might be called the grace of God. My spiritual growth has entailed becoming stronger in my faith. Just as I know the seasons will change, I know I can trust this divine grace and guidance to assist me in my ever-growing, and, hence, happier and more fulfilled soul.

CHAPTER 15

DIFFERENT PERSPECTIVES

Like horses wearing blinders on both sides of their heads, we tend to see only what is directly in front of us. To see anything else, we must pause, turn our heads, and look in another direction. Although we can never live anyone else's life, we can suspend our judgements and broaden our understanding by making the effort to look around, gather more information, and consider another person's point of view. The poet, John Godfrey Saxe expressed our limited perspectives best in his poem, "Blind Men and the Elephant":

> It was six men of Indostan,
> To learning much inclined,
> Who went to see the Elephant
> (Though all of them were blind),
> That each by observation
> Might satisfy his mind.
>
> The *First* approach'd the Elephant,

And happening to fall
Against his broad and sturdy side,
At once began to bawl:
"God bless me! but the Elephant
Is very like a wall!"

The *Second*, feeling of the tusk,
Cried, -"Ho! what have we here
So very round and smooth and sharp?
To me 'tis mighty clear,
This wonder of an Elephant
Is very like a spear!"

The *Third* approach'd the animal,
And happening to take
The squirming trunk within his hands,
Thus boldly up and spake:
"I see," -quoth he- "the Elephant
Is very like a snake!"

The *Fourth* reached out an eager hand,
And felt about the knee:
"What most this wondrous beast is like
Is mighty plain," -quoth he,-
"'Tis clear enough the Elephant
Is very like a tree!"

The *Fifth*, who chanced to touch the ear,
Said- "E'en the blindest man
Can tell what this resembles most;
Deny the fact who can,
This marvel of an Elephant
Is very like a fan!"

The *Sixth* no sooner had begun
About the beast to grope,

Then, seizing on the swinging tail
That fell within his scope,
"I see," -quoth he,- "the Elephant
Is very like a rope!"

And so these men of Indostan
Disputed loud and long,
Each in his own opinion
Exceeding stiff and strong,
Though each was partly in the right,
And all were in the wrong!

As in the case of the blind men in this poem trying to ascertain what an elephant is, we are more likely to gain a fuller picture of the nature of something, albeit an animal, a situation, or a moral principle, if we pull together everyone's ideas and perspectives. We may find where everyone is "partly in the right." With a fuller understanding of a bigger picture, we are more empowered to make good decisions. In addition, we can appreciate everyone who is contributing to the creation of this bigger picture, rather than dismiss each other or engage in a combative argument.

When we consider others' perspectives and ideas, we find the truth is rarely, if ever, this or that. Rather, it is this and that and more, just as an elephant cannot be defined by only his ear or his tail, but only by the sum of his parts. In addition, we may find that one elephant does not represent all elephants. Although they may be similar in appearance, elephants can vary a great deal in behavior and personality, depending on each elephant's circumstances and experiences.

When we earnestly seek to understand a mystery, we rarely find the answer to be black or white. Normally, it is as gray as an elephant. There is ambiguity and multiple dimensions and angles. The best we can do is search for all the clues we can find, then piece them together like a puzzle wherever they fit. Most likely, there will be missing pieces and more to learn. However, the more we learn the better we understand what we know and what we do not know, and what we know can lead us toward making better choices. As Charles Maurice Davies wrote, "The mind being forewarned is forearmed."

Anyone who believes they have all the answers in regard to the spiritual realm is delusional. No one can know it all. Although I believe we are connected to the same divine universal energy, and we can gain wisdom and guidance through our own intuitive or sixth sense, we cannot know all there is to know. This divine universal energy is far greater than the sum of its parts. It is an unsolvable mystery. As human beings, we have yet to learn all there is to know about what exists within the greatest depths of the oceans. How, then, can anyone claim to know all that exists within the depths of the universe? We can speculate what might be there. We can claim there are spiritual laws or deities, and we can ponder our paranormal experiences. However, all we can know for certain is whether any conviction we may possess is helping us to be our most authentic and loving selves. The proof is in our choices, our behaviors, and their corresponding outcomes. Each of our lives is a unique spiritual journey—a personal adventure of exploration and discovery. As we strive to find the clues to the wonders of life, we grow in knowledge and wisdom. The hidden treasures we seek are intangible. They cannot be seen or touched. They can only be felt deep inside of us where the energy of our souls reside. These treasures are immeasurable, inexplicable, and priceless.

We can discuss our experiences, but there is no use in trying to persuade or convert anyone to our interpretation of them. Therefore, I suggest we embrace an eclectic approach to our spiritual journeys. Enjoy our own experiences, and welcome our fellow travelers whenever and wherever we meet. Listen to each other's stories and what they have come to mean to us, and be open to new inspiration. We need not agree on anything. But, when we listen with the intention to understand, we might find more common ground than we had anticipated and experience a connection with each other that transcends the ordinary and becomes part of the flow of divine inspiration—a wonder no less than the universe itself.

C HAPTER 16

TRUST-FALL INTO THE UNIVERSE

Survey studies have shown Americans' number one fear is public speaking. This certainly had been true for me during my childhood, but my fear ran much deeper. I was afraid of speaking in general. I was afraid of people in any situation. During my school days, I dreaded encountering my classmates. I was absolutely silent during class, I avoided eye contact, and when I walked in the halls, I kept my head down and looked at the floor in the hope that no one would speak to me. Every fiber and nerve in my body became tense anytime anyone came near me, like a rabbit must feel toward its numerous predators. None of my peers had ever hurt me, and I wanted to make sure it stayed that way. I was called shy. I was called a wallflower. Sometimes, I was called a snob because I would not talk with anyone. But, for the most part, no one had even noticed me, which was the way I liked it.

To this day, I am not certain why I was so inflicted with social anxiety, except for the fact that I had no self-worth. I was certain that if others knew me, they would not like me, and worse, they would humiliate me, causing my already fragile self-esteem to break. Living in my own skin was too much of a burden as it was.

I nearly had a mental breakdown when my seventh-grade English teacher forced us to stand in front of the class and recite a monologue, "All the World's a Stage," from Shakespeare's play, *As You Like It.* Mrs. Proctor was a middle-aged woman who easily took command of the class. I admired her knowledge and her way of explaining literature. I loved her colorful way of expressing herself. I learned the meaning of the word, "parasite," when she used it to scold a classmate when she discovered he had someone else do his homework for him. She said, "Do you know what a parasite is, young man? Do you?" He shook his head to indicate he did not know. She continued, "Well, sir, you should know, because you are one. A parasite feeds off someone else. He doesn't do anything for himself. He takes, takes, takes, and never gives back. Is that how you want to be? Do you want to keep living that way, or do you think it might be a better idea to do your own work and be someone respectable?"

I felt a great respect for this teacher, but I was also a little afraid of her. She was stern, and she took no prisoners. So in addition to my usual fear of being humiliated by my peers, I was afraid if I did not do a good job when it was my turn to stand in front of the class, they would also learn a new word at my expense.

I practiced the assigned monologue repeatedly when I was alone in my bedroom. I recited it in the shower. I recited it when I was cleaning the house. I memorized "All the World's a Stage" to the point where I was dreaming it. I knew it as well as I knew my own name. I was sure I had every line down. The dreaded day for my turn to recite it in front of class came, and although I was certain I knew all the lines, I was so nervous I thought I might vomit when the moment arrived. I slowly walked to the front of the class and stood there, looking out at my classmates. I tried to speak, but the words refused to come out. Everyone waited, silently. Finally, I spoke. Then I babbled, blurting out such nonsense I didn't even know what I was saying. The classroom erupted into laughter. I felt faint and nearly collapsed. I must have been in a very sorry state, because our teacher, that very stern and scolding woman, took pity on me and came to my rescue. Mrs. Proctor put her arm around my shoulder, and slowly walked me back to my seat. She reassured me, saying, "You're okay. Calm down. You're okay. Take your seat. You're safe now."

I managed to regain my composure as I returned to my silent solitude, my proverbial cave, my safe hermitage, and the other children left me alone.

I didn't understand then that my fear of failure had caused me to fail. I hadn't yet figured out that the very thing we fear most we draw to us. The horrific experience in that moment in front of the class had been a self-fulfilled prophecy. My fear came from the belief that my classmates would humiliate me, and what we believe to be true has a great tendency to become true.

What if I had believed the opposite? What if I had believed my classmates would applaud me instead of laugh at me? Would my experience have been different? Yes, most definitely, as I learned many years later during my adulthood when I became a regular public speaker.

As with anything else we do, to learn something, we must first choose to learn. To love, we must first choose to love. To experience miracles, we must first choose to believe they are possible. When we understand the power of our beliefs to create our realities, we are motivated to take charge of our beliefs, examine them, and deliberately choose to possess beliefs that will help us rather than harm us.

Imagination can be very useful in changing our beliefs, as I discovered when I chose to conquer my fear of public speaking. I gave myself at least 30 minutes before I was to speak to meditate in a quiet place. I imagined myself feeling cheerful and confident. I imagined my audience, interested and engaged. In my mind's eye, I saw them smiling at me and nodding their heads. I told myself this experience would be a fun and interesting cocktail party. I told myself everyone in the audience was a friend. They would happily welcome me. We would enjoy each other's company. When the time came to get up on that stage, I had convinced myself this was going to be fun, and, every time, it was, so much so, that several members of the audience stayed after my speech to ask more questions and continue the conversation, just like good friends at a cocktail party.

Learning to believe in super-natural love works the same way. Imagine you are surrounded by a strong group of close friends who are determined to catch you when you fall into their arms. Then, take that leap of faith. Trust-fall into the Universe. Choose to believe the divine universal energy will catch you, and it will. The more you trust the divine, the more it will protect you, guide you, and help you to create the reality you need and want.

Believe you are loved, and you will experience love. Choose to become a vessel of love for yourself and others, and you will be filled with love and all the gifts it brings—joy, good health, peace, and abundance. To give love a chance, give faith in love a chance. If your fears are blocking you from making this choice, then choose first to conquer your fears. You can do it. Rather than predicting bad things will happen, predict good things will happen. Imagine the good.

You are the prophet fulfilling your own prophecy. Why? How? The divine universal energy lives within you and everyone else. We share this energy just as we are breathing the same air. All we need to do is believe in it, trust it, call upon it, and choose to live in harmony with it.

No, we cannot change others. We cannot make choices for others. We all have free will. However, we can make our own choices, and the choices we make can make all the difference. If you don't like the way the world is dancing, change the way you dance. Those who like the way you dance will choose to dance with you. That's really all we can do, and it's all we really need.

ABOUT THE AUTHOR

Lark Syrris

Lark Syrris lives in the Chicagoland area with her husband Demitri and their mini pinscher Chihuahua Triceratops (aka, Cera). She is recently an empty nester who now finds time to return to her passion for writing when she is not working as a  counselor at the local police department. During her career of the last 18 years working with men and women who have been victims of violent crimes, Lark Syrris has found herself increasingly amazed by the healing power of unconditional positive regard and spiritual insights. She draws her inspiration for her writing from her clients, her family, and her own spiritual quest and experiences. She believes her life's calling is to be a source of inspiration, hope and healing. Lark Syrris has an MA degree in English from Northern Illinois University, and an MS degree in Human Services from National-Louis University. She is a Licensed Clinical Professional Counselor (LCPC).

Before changing her career to the field of psychotherapy (also known by the friendlier term "counseling"), Lark Syrris had worked in the technical writing field, where she honed her writing skills to make complex subjects easy to understand. She entered this profession after reading Zen and the Art of Motorcycle

Maintenance by Robert Pirsig, which convinced her to give computer technology a chance, even though she had never seen a computer outside the Pac Man game that people played in bars. Serendipitously, she landed a job with Pirsig's former employer where Pirsig had been working as a technical writer by day and writing Zen and the Art of Motorcycle Maintenance by night. Lark Syrris knew from this moment of synchronicity that her fate as a technical writer had been sealed, but it would not end there.

Photo Credit: Victoria Lunacek Photography